DANCING

IN YOUR SCHOOL

DANCING
IN YOUR SCHOOL

A Guide for Preschool and Elementary School Teachers

ANNE DUNKIN

PRINCETON BOOK COMPANY, PUBLISHERS

Copyright ©2006 by Princeton Book Company, Publishers
All rights reserved

Princeton Book Company, Publishers
614 Route 130, Hightstown, NJ 08520
www.princetonbookcompany.com

Design, composition and drawings by John McMenamin

Library of Congress Cataloging-in-Publication Data

Dunkin, Anne.
    Dancing in your school: a guide for preschool and elementary school teachers /
    Anne Dunkin.
        p.cm.
    Includes bibliographical references.
    ISBN 0-87127-285-7
    1. Dance—Study and teaching (Elementary school) 2. Teachers—In-service training. 3.
Interdisciplinary approach in education. I. Title.

GV1589.D86 2006
372.86—dc22   2006045185

Also in the School Physical Activity Series:
Yoga In Your School by Teressa Asencia

6 5 4 3 2 1

CONTENTS

AGE-APPROPRIATE DANCE ACTIVITIES, SAMPLE LESSON PLANS, AND GROUP DANCES

All activities, lesson plans, and dances can be varied
in complexity to work for age groups other than the listed designation.

Pre-Kindergarten/Kindergarten

Kindergarten/through Third Grade

Third Grade and Older

ACKNOWLEDGEMENTS

Throughout several decades working as a dance educator in the United States, I have had the privilege to meet and work with hundreds of elementary school teachers. I am continuously awed by the ingenuity, passion, and perseverance that I have observed guiding their work, sometimes in the most inhospitable of places. It is with deep appreciation for and recognition of what they taught me by demonstrating what could occur in school settings that I have prepared this text and dedicated it to all teachers. This book includes activities, lesson plans, strategies, and approaches that have evolved from those experiences. Consequently many individuals have inspired and contributed to this text.

Following its initial inspiration, preparing a book for publication is a collaborative effort not unlike implementing a successful dance lesson or choreographing a dance. I wish to acknowledge my debt to those who have contributed their time and expertise to this particular endeavor. For reviewing and commenting on earlier drafts and chapters I thank arts educators Sallie Mitchell, Ph.D., California State University, Fullerton, and Cris Guenter, Ed.D., California State University, Chico; dance educators Barbara Bashaw, M.A., C.M.A., New York University, and Darline Ocadiz, M.A., California State University, Fullerton; classroom teachers Laura Hisrich, M.A.T., Eugene, Oregon, and Chris Roberts, M.A., Spanish Fork, Utah; and National Dance Education Organization Executive Director Jane Bonbright, Ed.D., and Project Director Rima Faber, Ph.D. Additionally I am most appreciative of the efforts of my publisher Charles Woodford and his staff at Princeton Book Company for their interest, guidance, and support throughout this process. Finally I extend my deepest thanks to my life partner, Brad Willis, not only for all the hours he spent helping to edit, proofread, and format this document but also for his unwavering support of all my dancing ventures for so many years.

INTRODUCTION

Dancing in Your School is a guide for preschool and elementary school classroom teachers as well as teachers of dance, music, and physical education, to integrate dance education into their curriculum. Its ultimate objective is that teachers develop their own dance lesson plans. It illuminates the value of dancing as a means to further learning by connecting aspects of established and mandated curriculum, developing critical thinking skills, and providing enjoyable learning experiences. It also introduces dance as arts education, which is a core subject area. Not only does this guide link dance activity with standards-based learning but also it discusses rationales for including dance in education—information that teachers can use to advocate the benefits of dance in education to administrators and parents.

This book provides strategies for class control and notes how teachers resolve the issue of space by using many settings: classrooms, cafeterias, all–purpose rooms, gymnasiums, vestibules, and outdoor areas.

A teacher does not have to be a dancer to facilitate these lessons. The approach is to engage students in a creative dance process where dancing creatively (rather than performing dance technique perfectly) is the objective. As they often do with other subject areas, teachers may wish to hone their skills further and consult dance specialists to provide additional experiences for their students and themselves.

We are going to take a joint adventure with your students as we all work together to create dance activities, expand movement vocabularies, develop critical thinking skills, and become familiar with dancing as a creative and expressive art. We will make and validate choices. You will demonstrate different choices and encourage your students to consider alternatives. We will use music and other arts expressions to enhance our activities.

We will also consider both the history of and rationales for dance in education settings. We will make connections between dancing and physical education, kinesthetic reinforcement of classroom learning, cultural play, and arts education. We will explore different learning and teaching styles for ourselves and our students, and we will assume and assign roles as observers, creators, performers, reflectors, and assessors of this process.

Throughout our quest we will use the elements of dance—body, space, time, and energy—to describe activities. We will use such descriptors both to compare one dance movement with another and as our tools to create movement variations. Our adventure will be at its best when you use your own creativity to invent dance activities and lessons derived from provided examples. As you gain confidence in your own ability to create dance lesson plans, you will also enhance your students' developing creative and learning skills.

The first seven chapters concentrate on dancing in school settings. They provide background information, specific introductory activities, and rationales for including them. The remaining four chapters address the role of the teacher as observer, creator of complete dance lesson plans, facilitator, and assessor.

The format of the text is designed for user-friendly reading. Illustrations are used to clarify movement descriptions as needed, and specific activity instructions appear in boxes. This allows for easy location when flipping through the book looking for single activities rather than rationales or background information on the subject. Appendices provide equipment and resource suggestions to enhance activities, dance education networking contacts, and additional lesson plan sources. A list of activities, sample lesson plans, and group dances described in this book precedes this chapter.

In every chapter I have placed italicized comments of former students, both adults and children, regarding their dance in education experience. I think they are quite insightful from their less-experienced vantage point.

ONE

Dancing In Your School

I learned that dance can bring us all together no matter our background.
We can all learn new ways to dance together.

> *First grade teacher*

Dancing activity introduces the values of keeping physically fit and practicing good health care. It also reinforces motor and physical development. It strengthens perceptual motor learning by fine-tuning kinesthetic awareness and students' responsiveness to their spatial and temporal surroundings. In the absence of a physical education specialist, pre-school and elementary classroom teachers may be expected to provide whatever structured physical exercise opportunity their students receive.

Dancing is physical education.

Through dancing activities students use different modes of learning and acquire knowledge experientially as will be shown in this book. Dancing can also connect different curricula areas such as learning a dance from a particular culture as part of a social studies unit, or studying vocabulary words by creating a dance illustrating the movement qualities of each word.

Dancing can kinesthetically reinforce classroom learning within the curriculum.

As students collaborate together on their dance expressions, they share each other's previous experience and create new learning together. They make both individual and group choices: social, cultural, and artistic. In the process of "trying on" and "experimenting with" their new learning, students discover different perceptions of their own identities.

Dancing engages students in cultural play.

Dancing provides arts education. Students experience dance as an art-making process. They see dance as its own subject, encouraging individual and group creative and artistic expression. Dancing also involves using and appreciating other arts expressions: music, visual, and dramatic arts.

Dancing provides arts education.

1

Good dance activities and lesson plans incorporate aspects of all four rationales. Students realize that with creative expression there are multiple possibilities. They are not looking for a right or wrong answer, but rather possible alternative solutions to presented problems. They expand their aural, visual, and kinesthetic senses. They listen to music and sounds that are unfamiliar. They experience a familiar subject by accessing contrasting visuals and diverse literary forms. They expand movement and verbal vocabularies by moving like and expressing dissimilar images through movement and sound.

My objectives are to integrate the core subject areas, arts, dance, music, and physical education into the curriculum. Students are able to learn in a way that allows them to use multiple tools to answer the same questions.

Fourth grade teacher

T W O

Dancing in School Settings

I do not remember learning about dance when I was in elementary school.
I see how much fun my students have in my class using dance to learn;
so I know that dance is an important part of the students' lives.

      Third grade teacher

Dancing in school settings is not a new idea. Even though many preschool and elementary teachers today did not participate in such activities during their own schooling, master's theses and doctoral dissertations as early as the 1930s have advocated the integration of dance activity into public school curriculums.[1] Throughout history dancing has been considered relevant to one's education for such reasons as pursuit of good health, development of the physical body, cultivation of the mind, acquisition of social skills, transmission of cultural traditions, and aesthetic development. Despite evidence that dancing activity is considered a significant aspect of one's education in many places throughout the world,[2] dance education has been found in private school settings more often than in public education facilities in the United States. Such disparity between theory and practice only reinforces a long-standing ambivalent relationship between public education in the United States and dance.

One practical aspect of this ambivalence may be the physical space needed for dance activities. Preschool and kindergarten classrooms are often larger rooms that can accommodate open space activities such as dancing, but classrooms for older students (who are also physically larger) are usually too full of desks for open space activities. If larger rooms such as gyms, all-purpose rooms or cafeterias are not available, teachers of older students must either move desks out of the way or modify their classrooms to accommodate some open space at either end or in the middle of the classroom. Teachers who do a lot of cooperative learning have reported using tables rather than desks which are easier for students to move out of the way.[3]

Historical Perspective [4]

1900–1960   The early twentieth century saw aspects of dance instruction in several schools and colleges in the United States. Those programs, identified as physical exercise, were housed in women's physical education departments (where, incidentally, lack of physical space was not usually a problem). Physical education had officially been part of public education since the time of the Civil War, and had organized itself as a professional domain in 1885 with the establishment of the American Association for the Advancement of Physical Education.

At the turn of the twentieth century additional factors, besides the importance of maintaining good health through exercise, influenced the dance syllabus that developed within the physical education curriculum.[5]

- Waves of new immigrants to the United States stimulated interest in folk and national or cultural dances as new populations assimilated with society. Folk dancing became an acceptable and popular form of physical education activity for young people, especially girls.

- Isadora Duncan and other pioneering dancers were drawing attention to new dance forms. Their dance practices, often identified as "aesthetic" and "natural," emphasized individual expression and interpretation. They utilized freer flowing movements such as walking, running, and leaping rather than stressing the perfection of recognized dance steps and routines. Although movements of these dance forms might include modifications of traditional ballet and folk dance steps, they all, to some extent, blended freer expression with harmonious and coordinated movement of the body.

- Progressive education "learning by doing" teaching methods advocated by John Dewey and Columbia University Teachers College were attracting attention in education. The philosophies of progressive education worked well with the values of folk dancing and the expressive dance forms of Isadora Duncan and other pioneering dancers. As a result, during the first three decades of the century, physical education students at Columbia University

Teachers College also studied dance. Several of those students became leaders of dance education in the United States, and established models for its implementation at different universities and in public school systems. One of the most notable of these was Margaret H'Doubler, who founded the first university dance major program at the University of Wisconsin in 1926.

The twentieth century saw multiple pendular swings in the field of education which impacted the presence of dancing activity in the schools. Generally the swing moved along a continuum from experimental and progressive ideas at one end to traditional and "back to basics" theories at the other.

Dance in education as an artistic or aesthetic pursuit finds more support on the experimental end of the education pendulum swing, and dance as a physical education activity promoting fitness and stamina resides at the traditional end.

A more conservative-thinking period in the mid-twentieth century— coupled with recovery from the great depression in the 1930s and World War II in the 1940s—followed the earlier progressive strides in education. During this time dance activity, when it existed, remained in physical education programs and often there was limited, if any, emphasis on its creative or aesthetic expression aspects.

The 1960s was a decade of contrasts that challenged public education to explore new directions which also influenced the history of dance in education.

1960–2000

- Desegregation and then integration of the public schools by court order in 1954 was followed by civil rights movements in the 1960s that redefined not only the place of African-Americans, but also that of women, gay men and women, and all minority populations in American society. In education, this involved focusing on student diversity in cultural backgrounds, academic accomplishment, and curriculum planning.

- The Soviet Union's success with launching the satellite Sputnik in 1957 resulted in greater emphasis on science and mathematics training in the United States. This influenced renewed interest in "back to basics" learning in classrooms which at first appeared to weaken progressive education ideals.

- In 1965 the federal government became actively involved with public education through two major pieces of legislation. As part of the "war on poverty," the Elementary Secondary Education Act (ESEA), which would be reauthorized every four years, designated funds to specifically target economically and "educationally deprived" students. Subsequent funding also focused on special needs students including gifted students and innovative teaching projects. Dance education profited because these funding areas incorporated allocations that could be used to provide dance and arts activities as enrichment experiences for these students. Developing dance curriculum benefited further from the funds designated to explore new teaching methods because many educators considered dance in the schools to be innovative. Additionally, in 1965, Congress established the National Endowments for the Arts and for the Humanities. This legislation renewed interest in arts education and provided funding for artists and arts specialists to go into the schools to provide arts experiences for students.

Increased government funding for education and arts programs[6] along with a national focus on diversity helped fuel a dance boom in the United States from 1965 to 1980. This led to subsequent growth of dance education and dance in education.

- More university dance degree programs developed, which in turn led to greater numbers of dance students attaining higher academic degrees.

- Many university dance programs shifted from physical education to arts affiliated departments, which placed greater emphasis on the creative and aesthetic aspects of dance education. This shift was affected in part by the passage of Title IX (part of ESEA) in 1972 and the Equal Educational Opportunity Act in 1974 that merged men's and women's physical education programs. These realigned programs often appeared to emphasize athletics rather than dance.

- Universities identified cultural studies as an important academic discipline and often incorporated dance within that context. This reinforced examination of the dance practice as a source for historical and anthropological study.

- The field of special education had gained significant recognition, and research identifying learning disabilities was actively pursued. Much of this research related learning with moving, and dance educators became involved and interested.

- By the 1980s and 1990s, education theory not only acknowledged potential differences in learning styles for all students, but was nurturing critical thinking skills as alternatives to rote memorization. Many of these new directions incorporated learning through and about the arts including dance.

Paradoxically, funding for many arts activities including dance diminished during the 1980s. However, different paths for the advancement of dance education were charted. Besides offering more advanced level university degrees in dance, the last half of the twentieth century defined both the value and the place for dance in K–12 education.

The 1994 Congressional legislation, Goals 2000–Educate America Act, reinforced the place of dance in K-12 education by embracing several components:

- The arts, including dance, were to be considered core curriculum for all students.
- Funding was allocated to ascertain curriculum content standards in the arts for all students.
- Guidelines for teacher certification in the arts needed to be established.

As a result of this legislation, curriculum content standards were developed for the arts in education. The Consortium of National Arts Education Associations developed *The National Standards for Arts Education: Dance, Music, Theatre, and Visual Arts.*[7] Additionally, the National Dance Association, along with music, theatre, and visual arts consortium members published stand-alone documents of their respective standards.[8] To date forty-nine states have adapted or adopted state arts standards based on the national model.

The four-year reauthorization of the Elementary and Secondary Education Act **No Child**
(ESEA), also known as the No Child Left Behind Act of 2001, was signed **Left Behind Act**
into effect in January 2002. This legislation called for high levels of academic accountability in "core subject areas" to be taught by "highly qualified" teachers. The arts were included as "core academic subjects."

Although advances had been made prior to this legislation toward creating dance curriculum content standards and establishing public school dance specialist teaching credentials, implementation of this legislation, which could determine federal funding for individual school districts, caused varying responses at both national and state levels. Many of these responses affected dance education and school teachers teaching dance. For example, the push for academic accountability was interpreted by many as a need to focus on testing and spending time preparing for tests. For many this translated into less class time for arts and physical education activities. Physical education programs felt additional concern because physical education had not been listed as a "core academic subject."[9] With specific reference to the arts, states could decide which arts might be core in their state. States without mandated dance content standards and assessments in place might easily focus on arts other than dance to implement the legislation. States could identify which teachers needed to be "highly qualified" as well as define what criteria determined "highly qualified." States without dance teaching certification might be unable to accredit highly qualified dance specialist teachers.

Contemporary Context

At the turn of the twenty-first century the reality of dance programs in public education was reflected in the 1999-2000 United States Department of Education report regarding arts education in public elementary and secondary schools. It ascertained that the comprehensive dance programs were usually found at the secondary and sometimes middle school levels.

The study located dance instruction in only twenty percent of the country's elementary schools, and of those offering dance instruction, forty-one percent were taught by the classroom teacher.[10]

More often than not dance education in elementary education has been dependent on the efforts of individual administrators, teachers, and/or parents who volunteered their time or secured outside funding to make the program happen.

These study findings underscore the significance of elementary teachers taking the opportunity to introduce dance education to their students. In elementary classes dance education can be a link to other curriculum areas at the same time that it enhances the development of the whole child. It can also be an important step toward many students choosing more specialized dance and arts focus at the middle or secondary school levels.

The elementary school teacher, usually not a dance-trained specialist, often becomes the first dance teacher for many students. As noted earlier in this chapter, dance activity may occur in a classroom with desks or tables pushed aside, a multi-purpose room, gymnasium, cafeteria/lunchroom, or outdoor setting. There are no mirrors, barres, or other dance studio furnishings.[11] There is no changing into dance attire; usually students wear clothes they wore to school that day.[12] Dancing in preschool and elementary classes is designed to involve all class members, the class as a whole, unless there is an individual health or ideological concern that prevents a student from participating. This also includes all mainstream special education and physically challenged students in the class.[13]

To successfully implement dance activity it is important to consider the physical, cognitive, and social benefits for students. These include:

**Goals for
Facilitating Dance
Education**

- Experiencing dance as an expressive and creative art form
- Understanding the value of physical fitness
- Developing an appreciation for dance
- Linking academic subject matter with arts education and physical education
- Developing communication and collaborative skills
- Reinforcing spatial and temporal relationships
- Connecting with cognitive learning through physical movement
- Developing creative thinking and problem-solving skills
- Fostering understanding of historical and cultural contexts

When students achieve these goals they greatly enhance their potential for successful participation in the world at large.

A purpose of this book is helping teachers to acquire skills in creating and developing their own artistic processes and dance activities. Integral to this procedure, teachers help students create their own activities.

**Curriculum and
Standards**

As cited earlier there are dance content standards to serve as guidelines to support teachers' dance knowledge and experience. In addition to the *National Standards for Arts Education* (see note 7), and the *National Standards for Dance Education for K-12 students* (see note 8), the *Standards for Dance in Early Childhood* for ages 2-5 years[14] is also available. These documents identify specific dance performance and knowledge achievement goals for students. Each publication provides a framework for creating dance activities and assessing students' progress. As noted earlier, virtually every state has developed arts education standards which can be obtained on the individual state's department of education website. The activities and procedures described in this book can be used to fulfill objectives of the national standards for dance education for preschool and elementary school grades.

Although school dance activity may arouse a student's passion to pursue a career in dance, it is not the purpose of the preschool and elementary school teacher to develop gifted and talented professional dancers. Such training remains in institutions specializing in that preparation. However, through dancing activities at school, teachers may identify those with a talent for dancing, or students who would benefit from more specialized training. Teachers can then connect those students with schools specifically designed to nurture their talent. Chapter 11 discusses this further.

> I took the same lesson plan we used in dance class (dance education class for classroom teachers) and implemented it in my own classroom. This was a successful turnout. Every single student participated, even the ones who never participate in any activity. They were a little shy at first, but once we got into groups for the culminating activity, it was like someone turned on their power switch. The usually reserved students gained the opportunity to observe, participate, and share in the groups. They were able to learn from the experience and learn from each other.
>
> Fourth grade teacher

Notes for Chapter 2

1. In 2001 the National Dance Education Organization (NDEO) received funding for a three-year project from the United States Department of Education to identify and document dance education research from 1926 to 2003. Results from that study including details regarding advocacy for dance in education (since 1926) can be found in the publication, *Research Priorities for Dance Education: A Report to the Nation* published by NDEO in 2004.

2. See Chapter 5, page 59-60.

3. Karen Konrad, who teaches a primary multi-age class says, "I never let the issue of space get in the way...I have never been in a classroom that could not be modified quickly to allow kids to move...I may have to modify the form our movement takes. I have designed my own classroom to fit all of the movement we do. I have enough table space to sit twenty-four kids. I have literacy, science, and math centers, and a student library, but the center of the room is quite open. I have a small classroom so I opted not to have a teacher desk...I do my work at a table and store my things in a closet and filing cabinet...I have also worked out time with our P.E. teacher to use the gym when he is not using it...The biggest help I found is teaching the concept of 'self space' and 'general space.' This concept allows the children to be safe and productive regardless of the environment they are in ('My body can shrink or expand to fit the space I am in.')."

   Chris Roberts, who teaches a fourth/fifth grade class says, "I use the lunchroom after it is cleaned up each day... The acoustics are horrible and the floor is linoleum on concrete, but at least it is big... When I can't get that space I use what the school calls the 'vestibule' which is a carpeted space about twenty by forty feet. Whenever I move in my classroom it isn't too difficult because I use tables instead of desks... and they are easy to move out of the way."

4. For additional historical detail about dance in education see Kraus, *History of the Dance in Art and Education*, pp. 292-342.

5. For descriptions of dance practices and their settings in the United States from 1890 to 1920 with particular reference to the participation of women and girls see Tomko, *Dancing Class*.

6. For more detail regarding national support for arts education see Bonbright, "National Support of Arts Education: Linking Dance to Arts Education Reform."

7. Consortium of National Arts Education Associations. *National Standards for Arts Education: Dance, Music, Theatre, and Visual Arts.* (Reston, VA, 1994). http://artsedge.kennedy-center.org/teach/standards.cfm. Available for purchase through the National Dance Education Organization. See www.ndeo.org.

8. National Dance Association. (1994). *National Standards for Dance Education: What Every Young American Should Know and Be Able to Do in Dance.* Reston, VA.: AAHPERD. Also in 1995 *National Standards for Dance Education plus the Opportunity-to-Learn Standards for Dance Education* (2nd edition) Reston, VA: AAHPERD. The latest edition (1997) *National Standards for Dance Education and Opportunity-to-Learn Standards in Dance Education* is

available through www.aahperd.org. The National Dance Association is an association of the American Association of Health, Physical Education, Recreation, and Dance. Additionally in 2005 the National Dance Education Organization prepared *Standards for Dance Learning and Teaching in the Arts: Ages 5-18.* Available through www.ndeo.org.

9. American Alliance for Health, Physical Education, Recreation and Dance (AAHPERD) press release dated February 25, 2004, stated "the omission of some subjects such as physical education and health education has the potential to create unintended negative consequences—diminishing time and resources for subjects not identified as core."

10. National Center for Education Statistics (NCES), Office of Educational Research and Improvement, *Arts Education in Public Elementary and Secondary Schools: 1999-2000,* pp. 25, 27. The report also stated that fourteen percent of secondary schools offered dance. There was no specific data for middle schools.

11. Ibid, p. 27. Elementary schools offering dance reported using the following spaces: fourteen percent had a dedicated room with special equipment; four percent had a dedicated room with no equipment; fifty-eight percent used a gym, auditorium, or cafeteria; and twenty-two percent used regular classrooms. Also see National Dance Education Organization, *Professional Teaching Standards for Dance in Arts Education.* Among other aspects of teaching, this document outlines considerations of physically safe spaces to use for dance activities.

12. There are safety issues regarding shoes. Shoes that are not tied or securely fastened (sandals, thongs, clogs, or loafers, for example) may fall off, become flying missiles, or cause students to twist an ankle while moving because of the shoes' lack of support. When shoes do fall off, they might hit other students or cause them to trip. Hard-soled shoes are additionally dangerous because students may be hit by someone else's feet during kicking activities or moving on the floor in non-standing positions. Also hard soled shoes may not be allowed on gym floors if that space is available. Therefore, if possible, sneakers or similar tie-on soft soled shoes are best for these activities. Some dance educators who have control over the space they use (that is clean and splinter free) ask students to remove their shoes and socks. Although this solves the above considerations, there are states that require that students to wear shoes at all times at school.

13. This text does not directly address differently-abled students. Appendix B-2-c, p. 176, offers resources for including these students in dance activities.

14. National Dance Education Organization. 2003. *Standards for Dance in Early Childhood.* Bethesda, MD. Additional information: www.ndeo.org.

THREE

Dance Language

When people/teachers say "dance," some children are
frightened by the word. But I found my students love to
do the dance activities and talk about them for days after.

First grade teacher

Because some children hesitate to try dancing activities for fear of something new or preconceived ideas they have about dancing, some dance educators suggest calling "dancing" activities something other than "dance" to entice participation. Some educators use the term "movement education," many dance educators use the term "creative movement," and other teachers I know have coined their own descriptors such as "rhythm and think" or "motion awareness." Depending on the practitioner, there may be few or no differences among the activities these various descriptors represent.

Is It Moving or Is It Dancing?

"Movement education" appeared in the United States during the 1970s, and was a new approach to the physical education curriculum, particularly elementary physical education. The emphasis was on learning basic movement skills, achieving body awareness, and using student-centered activities to discover movement possibilities. This approach helped students enjoy movement activity while progressing developmentally within a non-competitive environment. The movement education approach had been influenced by modern educational dance, a system developed by Rudolf Laban,[1] and introduced several years earlier in the British primary schools. After leaving Germany in the 1930s Laban, a choreographer, dance teacher, and theorist, had relocated to England where he continued to work extensively with movement observation and movement education[2] while developing his movement notation system called Labanotation.®

Primary school teacher preparation programs in England included studying Laban's modern educational dance, which essentially prepared teachers to use dance elements as tools to help their students explore and create movement possibilities. Influenced by Laban's work, a movement education approach, exploring fundamental movement skills using discovery techniques, was developed by elementary physical education educators in the United States.[3] For many elementary physical education specialists, movement education (or movement exploration) still exists as a teaching strategy in elementary physical education programs to develop basic movement skills that will be useful in sports-activity skill acquisition.

Although some of the objectives of movement education appear similar to those of dance instruction, movement education activities in the United States are usually not referred to as dance.

So What Makes It Dance? On occasion students participating in dance sessions will ask, "When are we going to dance?" Or they might state, "This is only exercising."

Identifying movement activity as dance involves defining movement in terms of the four dance elements: body, space, time, and energy. The movement also intends to express something: a story, an idea, or feeling.

This may be confusing because all dancing is movement of some sort. However, many will argue that not all movement is dance, even though movement by its very nature involves some body filling space and time, and using some degree of energy. For example, if students move their bodies into a position to specifically reinforce or demonstrate understanding of a classroom subject—such as illustrating the alignment of planets in the solar system or individually forming shapes of alphabet letters—many would state that this is not dance.

However, if a student consecutively forms the letters of a word moving smoothly from one letter to the next using four slow beats for each letter as if writing in cursive, this arguably becomes a dance. Or if students demonstrate planets moving, their tempos varying and relationships shifting, that also becomes a dance.

Definitions of dance abound in dance theory books. For the purpose of defining dancing activities at school, it appears that students moving their bodies together and consciously changing their use of space, time, and energy as they express a shared objective or purpose, can be defined as dancing. This extends beyond randomly moving one's body.

Throughout this text, the term dancing rather than movement is used, because an underlying objective of this book is that students should know and acknowledge that they are dancing.

A final consideration regarding dancing in school is the distinction between learning pre-arranged dances and creative dance.

Dancing or Creative Dancing

Creative dance connotes the participant's active discovery or creation of a movement response rather than copying someone or learning a pre-arranged dance.

Although this book emphasizes creative dance activities and lessons, there will be occasions to teach students dances from other cultures or countries. Learning these dances and creating variations of them is discussed in Chapter 7.

Elements of Dance as Dance Language

Students and teachers who are not familiar with dance as a subject need a vocabulary with which to discuss and describe it.

The four major elements of dance used here to discuss dancing are **body, space, time,** and **energy.**[4] (The specific attributes of each element listed below and the terminology used are the results of multiple sources that I have compiled through my own dance experiences.)

Four Elements of Dance and Their Attributes

Body

Parts and Whole

The body is the moving instrument. What specific parts of it are moving? Does the body appear to be moving as a whole unit? What is the body's shape or contour? Is it curved, straight, open, closed?

Space

Personal Space (or self space)

The area we can reach in all directions from the center of our bodies. We often think of personal space as stationary; however, we maintain our personal space as we move about an area.

General Space (or shared space)
A designated area we travel in and share with others. This could be within the classroom, outdoors, or any other area.

Shape – Spatial formation and group configuration
Shapes may be concrete (lines, circles, squares) or abstract (nonspecific). They may be symmetrical or asymmetrical, open or closed, smooth or jagged. In surrounding space single bodies form shapes, bodies together form shapes, and also move in shapes.

Level – Low, Middle, High
Standing and walking is middle level for the body. Rising on one's toes and leaving the floor is high level. Bending one's knees and lowering to the floor is low level.

Direction – Forward, Backward, Right, Left, Diagonal
Refers to the direction the moving body travels or its individual parts moving in space.

Pathway – Straight, Curved, Zigzag
Describes the shape of the path the moving body travels in or its individual parts move.

Time

Duration
The length or amount of time used by the movement is its duration. This might be the length of a quarter note, or several seconds, or any specified amount of time.

Pulse
The steady, underlying beat of the movement or its musical accompaniment is its pulse.

Rhythm
A pattern of accented and unaccented beats creates the rhythm. This might be march rhythm, waltz rhythm, or any other patterning of beats.

Tempo

The rate of speed (tempo) of the movement or music describes how fast or slow it is.

Syncopation

An unexpected (uneven, erratic) accent in the movement or music is syncopation.

Energy

The amount and quality of the energy used by the movement is described by determining if the movement is:

Strong or Light

The amount of weight or force driving a movement determines if it is strong or light in quality. (Pushing a large box filled with books across the floor usually requires strong movement. Brushing a hair out of one's eyes is usually a light movement.)

Sudden or Sustained

The amount of time a movement lasts added to its speed determines its quality as sudden or sustained. (An unexpected usually quick movement is sudden. A slower continuous movement without variation in tempo is sustained.)

Direct or Indirect

The amount of space a movement uses describes the movement as direct or indirect. (A movement traveling in the shortest straightest path toward its destination is direct. A movement traveling a divergent meandering path to its destination is indirect.)[5]

Bound or Free Flow

The amount of tension in a movement describes its quality as bound or free flow. (A tighter restricted movement such as clenching a fist is bound flow. A looser or relaxed movement that moves easily such as extending an arm in friendship is free flow.)

All four elements (body, space, time, and energy) are involved in every dance movement, but all of their attributes, such as syncopation for example, may not be present. Depending on individual perception, one or two of the four elements may appear to be more dominant than the others, but all four are always present.

Developing familiarity with the elements of dance and the terminology with which to accurately describe them enables students and teachers to communicate during creative exploration and development of dance activities. Such facility further enhances verbal and written reflection following the activity.

Notes for Chapter 3

1. Laban, *Modern Educational Dance.*

2. Ann Hutchinson Guest, first a student and then colleague of Rudolf Laban in London, has spent a lifetime developing Laban's movement notation. She has expanded its use for the recording (notating) and reconstructing of dances as well as its applications in educational and therapeutic settings. Of particular interest to school educators is the use of some of the Labanotation symbols in Motif Description. This usage allows for a general description of the primary movement characteristics of a movement rather than a fully detailed documentation of the movement. Dr. Guest also created a method for building blocks of movement employing motif symbols and a basic movement alphabet called Language of Dance®. For more information on this method go to http://www.lodc.org/whatis.html.

3. I personally knew several educators (and dancers) from the United States who traveled to England during the 1970s to observe movement education programs in the British primary schools. One in particular, an elementary school principal who was quite impressed with the "use of movement in the British schools," indicated to me that he felt movement education was "not dramatic enough" to gain overwhelming popularity in the United States.

4 These four elements are borrowed from Rudolf Laban's model (see Note 1 above).

5. Barbara Bashaw, MA, CMA – Director of The Dance Education Program, New York University, The Steinhardt School, has suggested the following clarifications: direct movement is "a movement that channels the space such as poking, pin-prick, targeting. A movement that encompasses the space is indirect such as widening, including, enveloping." Email correspondence dated August 29, 2005.

FOUR

Dancing as Physical Education

The main reason I like to incorporate dance into my lessons is that most people, especially boys, don't like to dance because they have not done it. But once they have done it a few times, they like it, and I have a great opportunity to start with the young working on the elementary level.
        Elementary physical education instructor

The educational objectives shared by dance and physical education focus on the performance ability of the moving body. They include maintaining physical fitness and health, motor and physical development, and perceptual motor learning. These objectives appear in the dance content and achievement standards noted earlier in this book and in *National Standards for Physical Education*.[1] To appreciate the significance of these three aspects of physical movement, it is beneficial for teachers to physically move themselves and recognize how much better they feel as a result of adding physical exercise to their daily schedules.

I like to dance because it is fun and it is like exercise.
        Student, eight years old

Physical Fitness and Health

Interest in physical fitness and health remained strong throughout the twentieth century and into the twenty-first century. Daily we see joggers clocking their progress on city streets as other people hire personal trainers, join gyms, or attend exercise classes in pursuit of physically fit bodies. During the late twentieth century various types of aerobic dance became the popular choice of both men and women seeking physical fitness through an essentially non-competitive group activity. The use of music and rhythm was an important feature of aerobic dance as it motivated participants to follow and learn dance routines designed to increase flexibility and build strength and endurance. Many people consider aerobic dance and dance to be one and the same. Like all movement, aerobic dance does demonstrate the elements of dance: body, space, time, and energy, but its primary emphasis is the pursuit of physical fitness rather than providing channels for creative expression.

Despite visible impressions that many people strive to become physically fit, news media sources report that many children and young people are not passing basic physical fitness tests at school. Additionally, children are exhibiting signs of obesity and even heart disease and diabetes risk factors.

Such reports often identify the numbers of hours young people spend in front of television screens and computer monitors rather than participating in physical exercise activities. To further complicate matters, government and school administration budget cuts often eliminate elementary school physical education specialist teachers from school districts as well as funding for after-school activities. This particularly targets students who cannot afford to pay for participation in extra-curricular sports and dance activities.

Including dancing activities not only introduces and reinforces physical skills for students, but it also helps them learn that exercise, diet, and feeling physically good are important for living a healthy life.[2]

Activities demonstrating these concepts follow.

Activity 4-1
BODY WAKE-UP

Age:
All ages
Time:
2 or 3 minutes

Objectives:
To introduce feeling physically fit; to wake up bodies after sedentary activity; to warm up bodies for physical exercise and to prevent injuries.

1 2 3 4 5 6 7, 8 & 9 10 11 12 13

1. Stand in personal space.
2. Stretch body and arms straight to the ceiling.
3. Lower arms to sides of the body.
4. Smoothly roll head, neck, shoulders forward,
   curving down toward the floor.
5. Bending knees, roll the body, arms and legs into a ball shape
   close to the floor.
   Then
6. Slowly unfold body, straighten legs and stand tall.
7. Lunge forward on one leg, both arms out to the sides.
8. Bend front leg and stretch back leg pressing both heels into the floor.
9. Repeat with the other leg.
   Then
10. Run twenty-five seconds in place.
    Then
11. Perform five jumping jacks, opening legs to the sides
    clapping hands overhead.
12. Close legs together placing arms down alongside body.
13. Standing tall, inhale deeply through nose exhale slowly from mouth.

Learning Outcomes:
Students feel invigorated and learn the importance of warming up
before exercising to prevent injury.

Reversing the movements within Activity 4-1 and eliminating the running in place and jumping jacks portions provide a cool-down exercise.

Activity 4-2
BODY COOL-DOWN

Age:
All ages
Time:
2 or 3 minutes

Objective:
To cool down body after exercise.

1   2, 3 & 4   5   6   7   8   9   10   11

1. Standing tall, inhale deeply through nose exhale slowly from mouth.
   Then
2. Lunge forward on one leg, both arms out to the sides.
3. Bend front leg and stretch back leg pressing both heels into the floor.
4. Repeat with the other leg.
   Then
5. Stand tall.
6. Stretch body and arms straight to the ceiling.
7. Lower arms to the sides of the body.
8. Smoothly roll head, neck, shoulders forward, curving down toward the floor.
9. Bending knees, roll the body, arms and legs into a ball shape close to the floor.
   Then
10. Slowly straighten legs and straighten body.
11. Standing tall, inhale deeply through nose exhale slowly from mouth.

Learning Outcomes:
Students stretch out and relax tired muscles and prepare to return to more sedentary activity.

To become familiar with dance language, describe activities using the elements of dance and their attributes.

Activities 4-1 and 4-2 movement description

- Five *body parts* (arms, head, neck, shoulders, legs) and the whole body move(s) in *personal space*.
- The body forms tall, open, and closed ball *shapes*.
- The body moves through middle, high, and low *levels*.
- The body steps into forward, back, and side *directions*.
- Straight and curved *pathways* are used.
- There is variation in *tempo* between faster and slower movements.
- *Durations* of five jumping jacks and twenty-five seconds are designated.
- "Smoothly," "inhale deeply," and "pressing heels into the floor" describe *energy* used.

Describing physical exercises using attributes of the elements of dance introduces students to thinking about the form a particular movement takes. It also suggests additional movement possibilities and variations including the use of different body parts.

Activity 4-3
THE MOVING SPINE
CURVED AND STRAIGHT SHAPES

Age:
3rd grade/older
Time:
2 or 3 minutes

Materials:
Skeleton (see Appendix A-1, page 170)
Objectives:
To introduce a specific body part and create a movement
variation based on its range of motion. To introduce
stretching exercises that involve sequential rolling down
and up of the body's torso.

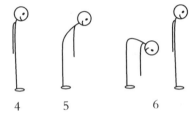

4   5   6

1. Students identify the skeleton's spine and vertebrae.
2. One student counts the seven cervical (neck) vertebrae by
   pointing to them.
3. Another student counts the twelve thoracic (to the waist) vertebrae.
   Then
4. All students stand tall and, counting seven counts, roll their heads and necks
   forward slowly (one count for each vertebra).
   Then
5. Continue rolling head, shoulders, and chest toward the floor, counting
   twelve counts (one count for each vertebrae).
   Then
6. Hanging over at the waist (not hip), top of the head facing the floor, roll up
   to standing counting again nineteen vertebrae beginning at the waist.

Learning Outcomes:
Students locate their spine and identify nineteen of its vertebrae. They become
aware of its movement capability. They recognize and experience straight and
curved body shapes.

Activity 4-3 movement description

- *Body* parts used are head, neck, shoulders, chest, rib cage, and waist.
- The upper body leads in a forward *direction* following a curved *pathway* from middle to low *levels*.
- The body moves from a straight to a curved shape and then returns to a straight *shape*.
- *Duration:* seven, twelve, and nineteen counts.
- *Energy* is *sustained* (continuous, slower unchanging tempo).

Using Activity 4-3 as an example, and referencing the skeleton as a model, it is possible to create exercises for other body parts based on their individual properties and range of motion.

Activity 4-4
HAPPY TOES, ANGRY TOES

Age:
Pre-K/K
Time:
2 or 3 minutes

Objectives:
To introduce movement variations and movement similarities for several body parts. To develop awareness of tension in the body.

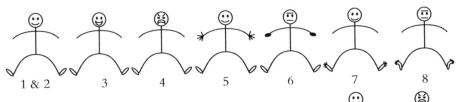

1. Sit on the floor with legs extended forward.
2. Arms and hands extended forward from the shoulders.
3. Show happy smiling faces.
4. Show angry scrunched faces.
   Then
5. Show happy smiling hands and fingers. (example: Fingers are open and spread apart.)
6. Show angry hands and fingers. (example: Hands form tight fists.)
   Then
7. Show happy smiling toes. (example: Separate toes [inside shoes if needed]. Spread them apart.)
8. Show angry toes. (example: Scrunch toes tightly [inside shoes].)
   Then
9. Show happy smiling whole bodies.
10. Show angry whole bodies.
    Then
Which feels better? Discuss answers.

Learning Outcomes:
Students distinguish tension and tightness versus relaxation in their bodies and how each feels. They relate this to physical fitness.

Activity 4-4 movement description

- *Body* parts are face, hands, feet, whole body.

- *Shapes* in personal *space* are open and closed.

- *Energy* is free and relaxed, and bound and tight *flow*.

Although this activity is designed for younger students, distinguishing tension and relaxation in one's body is important for all students and is an aspect of maintaining physical fitness and health. Variations of stretching exercises can be used to introduce physical fitness, to identify body parts, to warm-up/cool-down bodies, and relieve tension from sedentary activities. Regardless of specific objectives, when students focus on the condition of their bodies and feel differences between moving easily and not so easily, they begin developing lifelong habits associating physical movement activity with generally feeling better and keeping fit.

Motor and Physical Development

Motor and physical development of young people is another shared objective of physical education programs and dance activity.[3]

It has long been established that young children learn by physically moving in and around their environment.

A child who does not move well may be regarded by others as clumsy and uncoordinated. This child is often an unpopular child who is not readily selected by peers to be part of their team or group. These children sit alone on the playground and endure countless taunts of classmates. In my experience as a dance educator, I have noted that once children begin walking many parents neglect the pursuit of other motor skills such as galloping and skipping and focus instead on sedentary achievements such as early reading, for example. Learning and reinforcing developmentally appropriate motor skills is a recognized objective of the physical education domain, but it is also essential in dancing activity for young people. Acquisition of appropriate motor skills influences students' success not only with athletic and dance skills but also with social relationships and their ability to take advantage of lifelong activities.

For the purposes of physical education and dance activities, motor skills are divided into three types: **locomotor, non-locomotor,** and **perceptual motor**.

Locomotor skill includes visible body movements that move the body from one place to another. *Non-locomotor* movements are also visible but the body does not travel. *Perceptual motor* skill refers to movements of the body that may not be visible but which affect the five senses: seeing, hearing, touching, smelling, tasting. The first three of these—seeing, hearing, touching—are particularly important to physical education and dance education, because they directly affect balance, physical coordination, and spatial and temporal orientation.

There are eight basic locomotor (traveling) movement skills for children to master: walking, running, jumping, hopping, galloping, skipping, leaping, and sliding.

Most children entering kindergarten will be close to mastering these eight basic locomotor skills. However, it is not unusual to find upper elementary age students still experiencing difficulty performing them.

Walk (or step) – Complete shift of weight from one leg to the other traveling into any direction.

Run – A fast walk with one foot at a time momentarily leaving the floor.

Jump – Leaving the floor with both feet simultaneously; landing on both feet.

Hop – Leaving the floor with one foot and landing on the same foot.

Gallop – One leg leading, step-close-step pattern, with slight spring forward.

Skip – Stepping and hopping on one foot; repeat with other leg and foot.

Leap – A very big step rising off the floor from one foot, landing on the other foot.

Slide – One leg leading, step-close-step pattern, with slight spring sideward.

Mastering the eight traditional locomotor movements provides important building blocks for all students in terms of achieving later dance and sports abilities.

Do not assume that students can successfully perform locomotor movements, just because movements may be designated as developmentally appropriate. As indicated earlier, I have witnessed many upper elementary school age students as well

Locomotor Movement

Eight Locomotor Movements

Building Locomotor Movement Skill

as university students who are unable to skip and leap easily. Therefore it is essential to review and keep reinforcing fundamental locomotor skills with students before proceeding further.

The order of the following locomotor movement activities is according to the developmental acquisition of most children. In two of them, the movements are listed together: walking and running, and jumping and hopping.

1. Walking and running involve completely shifting weight from one leg to the other.

Activity 4-5
ONE LEG OTHER LEG
SHIFTING WEIGHT

Age:
Pre-K/K
Time:
1 to 2 minutes

Objective:
To reinforce complete shifting of weight from one leg to the other.

1. Practice walking, shifting weight from one leg to the other.
   Then
2. March in place, lifting one knee high in front and then the other.
   Then
3. Walk or march forward into general space, emphasizing the total shifting of weight.
   Then
4. Gradually increase tempo.
5. Walk faster and faster, gradually beginning to run.

Learning Outcomes:
Students comprehend and demonstrate completely shifting weight from one leg to the other while walking and running.

2. Galloping is performed with one leg leading the other. Many young children will begin galloping before or about the same time they begin to run.

Activity 4-6
GALLOPING

Age:
Pre-K/K
Time:
2 – 3 minutes

Objectives:
To identify galloping and develop skill performing it.

1. Encourage galloping in a circle.
   Then
2. Demonstrate one leg leading, the other following.
3. Keep changing leading leg until children are comfortable with both legs leading.
4. Gradually increase tempo.

Learning Outcome:
Students identify galloping and demonstrate it alternating the leading leg.

Most children by age three are walking, running, and galloping. When students are not performing these skills on their own, teachers can travel alongside holding the student's hands to reinforce the rhythm and weight shift in the movement.

3. Jumping and hopping skills must be acquired before skipping can be successfully mastered. Sitting on a large physioball and bouncing on it helps young children experience the steady rhythm of jumping before actually trying to jump. Also the image of a ball bouncing helps children connect with the concept of bouncing rhythm.

Activity 4-7
BOUNCE THE BODY (JUMP AND HOP)

Age:
Pre-K/K
Time:
2 to 3 minutes

Materials:
A large physioball
Objectives:
To experience a steady rhythm to prepare for jumping
and hopping. To practice both skills.

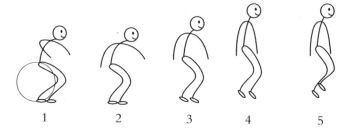

1   2   3   4   5

1. Bounce the body (example: Either sitting on a large ball held by teacher, or pretending to bounce a ball standing in place.)
   Then
2. Standing, begin bending the knees and tap pretend ball, straightening the knees as it releases. Verbalize "bounce your body," as legs bend.
   Then
3. Gradually begin jumping leaving the floor with both feet and landing on both feet. Verbalize "two feet" to "two feet" as students land.
   Then
4. Place arms alongside body as students jump higher.
   Then
5. When students understand they are using two feet, try hopping on one foot. Repeat using the other leg.
6. Students verbalize "one foot" to "same foot" as they hop taking off and landing on the same leg.

Learning Outcomes:
Students jump using both feet equally. Students distinguish jumping on two feet and hopping on one foot (same foot).

4. Skipping is difficult for some students, and may not occur before four and a half or five years of age.

Activity 4-8
STEP AND HOP (SKIP)

Age:
K/3rd grade
Time:
2 to 3 minutes

Objectives:
To progress from shifting weight, to marching in place, to step hopping, to skipping.

1. Marching in place lift one knee and hold it lifted.
2. Lower leg, step on it (shift weight) and lift the other knee. Hold it lifted. Repeat several times. Verbalize "step, lift."
   Then
3. Lift one knee and leave the floor (hop) on the supporting leg and land on the same supporting foot.
4. Repeat this on the other leg and foot.
5. Students verbalize "step, hop" emphasizing "step" as weight is shifted.
   Then
6. Quicken the tempo moving from one leg to the other.
   Then
7. Travel by skipping (step hopping) into general space.

Learning Outcomes:
Students identify skipping and demonstrate it using both legs.

---

5. Leaping can be performed by most children by five or six years old. Depending on their earlier movement experience, however, some may take longer to comprehend the movement and feel comfortable performing it.

Activity 4-9
LEAPING OVER

Age:
K/3rd grade
Time:
Varies (depending
on number
of students)

Materials:
Two ribbons (see Appendix A-2, page 170)
Objectives:
To experience leaping, taking a large step leaving the floor off one foot, traveling through the air, and landing on the other foot.

1   2   3   4   5

1. Place two pieces of ribbon on the floor to mark a "river."
 Then
2. Students (one at a time) jump over the river pushing off on two feet and landing on two feet.
 Then
3. Students (one at a time) hop over the river pushing off on one foot and landing on the same foot.
 Then
4. Students (one at a time) leap (or take a big step) over the river pushing off on one foot and landing on the opposite foot.
 Then
5. Keep increasing the distance between the two ribbons as students stretch their legs further.

Learning Outcomes:
Students distinguish jumping on two feet, hopping on the same foot, and leaping, using one leg for take-off and the other for landing.
They perform leaps alternating legs.

6. Sliding is similar to galloping, but it generally moves to the side instead of forward. Both movements, along with skipping, follow an uneven rhythmic pattern. Since moving to the side is usually difficult for young children, it is important that they be introduced to side movement at a young age; and the following Activity 4–10 using the instructions "step, step together, step" is a good way to do it. Once students are comfortable moving to the side, quicken the pace and say "step side, slide together."

Activity 4-10
STEP, STEP TOGETHER, STEP (SLIDE)

Age:
Pre-K/K
Time:
Varies (depending
on number
of students)

Objectives:
To master moving to the side and sliding.

1. Face the student and hold both his/her hands.
2. Step with one leg and foot to the side.
3. Move the other leg and foot next to it.
4. Verbalize "step side, step together, step side, step together."
   Then
5. Still holding student's hands, continue across the floor, gradually increasing tempo, adding a slight spring.
6. Repeat returning back across the floor leading with the other leg and foot.
   Then
7. Release hands. Facing student, place both hands on hips and slide across the floor facing each other.
   Then
8. Students slide facing other partners, first holding hands and then not holding hands.

Learning Outcomes:
Students identify sliding, and demonstrate sliding to the side without turning their bodies to the front or on the diagonal.

Generally, distinguishing right and left sides of the body is appropriate for six year old students. With younger students, or when there is still obvious difficulty moving to the side, practice side movements by emphasizing "one" leg steps to the "side" (demonstrate which one but do not identify as right or left). It is important for young children to feel comfortable moving to the side before they need to clarify which side is involved.

A more complex side movement called the grapevine, which crosses one leg in front or in back of the other leg, is developmentally appropriate for six and seven year old students. Because variations of this "crossing one leg over" step are found in most dance styles and folk dances, it is a useful step for students to learn.

Activity 4-11
CROSSING GRAPEVINE

Age:
1st grade/older
Time:
3 to 5 minutes

Objectives:
To cross one leg in front of and/or in back of the body while moving to the side.

1. Stand on both feet, weight centered.
2. Step to the right on the right foot.
3. Left foot steps in back of the right foot.
4. Step to the right on the right foot again.
5. Place the left foot next to the right foot, centering weight.
6. Encourage students to say the movements and directions as they perform them.
   Then
7. Repeat to the other side.
   Then
8. Repeat, crossing the leg in front.

Learning Outcome:
Students understand and demonstrate crossing legs in front of and/or in back of the body while moving to the side and without turning the body.

Once students can perform locomotor skills, practice them with Activity 4–12.

Activity 4-12
FOLLOW THE LEADER
LOCOMOTOR MOVEMENT

Age:
All ages
Time:
10 to 12 minutes

Objectives:
To practice locomotor movement skills. To reinforce using variations of the elements of dance and their attributes.

1. Continually changing leaders, move through general space and select different locomotor movements. (example: Run across the room.)
   Then
2. Older Students may vary body level, directions and pathways. (example: Bend knees, walk backward in a circular path.)
   Then
3. Add movement for other body parts. (example: Twist shoulders to one side. Open both arms to the sides of the body. Raise face to the ceiling)
   Then
4. Vary tempo and energy and energy expenditures. (example: Move quickly and lightly.)

Learning Outcomes:
Students strengthen locomotor skills, recognition and performance as they expand movement vocabulary.

Activity 4-12 movement description

- The *body* travels from one place to another.
- When traveling in general space, steps can move in all *directions* and on any *pathway*.
- The body usually moves in middle and high *levels*.
- Walking, running, leaping, jumping, hopping follow even *rhythmic* patterns.
- Skipping, galloping, and sliding utilize uneven *rhythmic* patterns.
- *Energy* and *tempo* changes can be specified.

Most young people enjoy performing locomotor movements, probably because of the freedom they feel and energy they are able to use when moving through space. However, these eight movements are just a beginning. Literally translating locomotor as traveling from one place to another, it is possible to think of endless numbers of movement possibilities besides variations of the eight basic locomotor movements.

Activity 4-13
TRAVELING FROM ONE PLACE TO ANOTHER

Age:
All ages
Time: Varies
(depending
on number
of students)

Objectives:
To think of different ways to travel through general space, and to create locomotor movement variations using the elements of dance and their attributes.

1. In partners, travel across the floor.
   Use the eight locomotor movements.
   Then
2. Older students create traveling movements other than the eight traditional ones. (example: Rolling on the floor; spinning)
   Then
3. Utilize all the attributes of the elements of dance to create different ways to travel.
4. Vary body part(s) that lead the movement. (example: Head pulls the body across the floor.)
5. Vary levels. (example: Walk on tiptoes.)
6. Vary direction and pathway. (example: Run forward in zigzag pathway.)
7. Change tempo and energy used for each movement. (example: Alternate moving quickly, slowly; loudly, softly.)
8. Try to be different from everyone else.

Learning Outcomes:

Students reinforce eight locomotor skills and other ways to travel across the floor. They create variations of locomotor movements using the elements of dance and their attributes.

Another type of movement, non-locomotor movement, does not travel from one place to another. These movements generally occur in personal space when the student is sitting, lying, or standing in one place. Non-locomotor movements may involve the whole body or single body parts.

**Non-Locomotor
Movement**

Activity 4-14
ING MOVING

Age:
3rd grade/older
Time:
10-15 minutes

Objectives:
To introduce non-locomotor movement using "ing" words, the present participle form of verbs, and to create non-locomotor movement variations.

1. Stand in personal space.
2. Without traveling, express each of the following "ing" words: rising, falling, widening, narrowing, advancing, retreating, pushing, pulling, bending, and straightening.
   Then
3. Try these movements with one body part, another body part, whole body.
   Then
4. Vary each, using different attributes of space. (example: Change level of the body or body part; move body part in directions away from and returning to the center of the body.)
   Then
5. Vary each, using different attributes of time. (example: Change tempo performing quickly or slowly; lengthen or shorten duration.)
   Then
6. Vary each, using different attributes of energy. (example: Repeat movements as suddenly, sustained, strongly, and lightly.)
   Then
7. Think of other "ing" words to express in movement.

Learning Outcomes:
Students understand non-locomotor movement. They expand movement and verbal vocabularies creating variations of non-locomotor movements using the elements of dance and their attributes.

Activity 4-15

TALKING GESTURES

Age:
K/3rd grade
Time:
5–10 minutes

Objectives:
To introduce gestures as non-weight bearing (non-locomotor) movements of the body. To create gestures that express feelings, ideas, sentiments.

1. Stand in personal space.
2. Students create gestures expressing happiness, anger, defiance. (example: Waving an arm to say hello, shaking a fist angrily, stomping a foot defiantly.)
3. Use single body parts.
4. Vary the body parts.
5. Vary level, direction, pathway of the gesture.
6. Vary tempo and energy for each gesture.
   Then
7. Think of other feelings, ideas, attitudes to express with gestures.

Learning Outcomes:

Students experience different meanings and feelings expressed by gestures. They use variations in the elements of dance and their attributes.

Perceptual Motor Learning

Perceptual motor learning[4] refers to a child's ability to take information in from the environment through all the senses, process it, and respond to it. These perceptions involve visual, auditory, tactile, balance, and proprioceptive or kinesthetic senses.

Part of successful perceptual motor learning involves acquiring a good sense of the whole body and its position in space.

This incorporates making neural connections within the body as well as with the surrounding environment.[5] The following are capabilities that assist children in making these neural connections.[6] Each of these can be reinforced through dancing activities which follow.

• Identification of body parts, edges (sides), and surfaces (front, back).

- Comprehension of moving in forward, backward, sideward, and diagonal directions.

- Ability to maintain personal space and also move in general space.

- Distinction of right and left (laterality) sides of one's own body.

- Recognition of directions including right and left outside of one's body (directionality).

- Crossing midlines of the body (sagital: right and left sides; transverse: upper and lower; frontal: front and back).

- Judging distance.

Activity 4-16
THE HOKEY POKEY

Age:
Pre-K/3rd grade
Time:
Varies (depending
on number and
age of students)

Music:
The Hokey Pokey
Objectives:
To identify body parts, edges, and surfaces.

1. Stand in a circle. Follow the lyrics.
2. "You put one hand in (the circle), you put one hand out (of the circle), you put one hand in and you shake it all about. You do the hokey pokey and you turn yourself around, that's what it's all about."
   Then
3. Substitute "other hand," "one foot," "other foot," "head," "whole self." Older students may name the hands and feet used, right hand, left foot, etc., while repeating the lyrics.
   Then
4. Going around a circle, each person moves a different body part.

Learning Outcomes:
Students identify body parts, edges, and surfaces. Students add to the activity by suggesting different body parts.

Activity 4-17
CHANGING DIRECTIONS

Age:
K/3rd grade
Time:
Age: 3–5 minutes

Music:
Drum (see Appendix A–20, page 173)
Objectives:
To move in forward, backward, sideward, and diagonal directions.

Younger children
1. Stand in personal space. Strike drum once for each change in direction.
2. Jump forward, backward, to one side, to the other side, diagonally forward and diagonally back to one side and then the other.
3. Students say the directions as they jump into them to reinforce comprehension.

Older students
4. Stand in personal space. Strike drum in counts of four or eight.
5. Students move around the room, changing direction every four or eight counts.

Learning Outcomes:
Students identify the different directions and move in them.

Activity 4-18
PERSONAL SPACE AND GENERAL SPACE

Age:
K/3rd grade
Time:
Age: 3–5 minutes

Music:
Drum (see Appendix A–20, page 173)
Objectives:
To introduce maintaining personal space and
moving in general space.

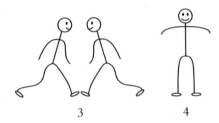

3   4

1. Teacher defines personal and general space (see pages 15 and 16).
2. Students perform any non-locomotor movement
   in personal space for eight counts.
   Then
3. Using a locomotor movement, they travel around the room
   for eight counts sharing the space with other students.
4. Return to personal space to recognize the difference.

Learning Outcomes:
Students define and comprehend the difference between personal and
general space. Students choose their own movements.

Activity 4-19
RIGHT OR LEFT
LATERALITY

Age:
K/3rd grade
Time:
3-5 minutes

Objectives:
To distinguish right and left sides (laterality) in their own bodies. To move to the right and to the left sides.

1. Place students behind teacher. Both face the same wall.
2. Move body parts of one side of the body and move to that side. (example: Lift right arm to the right side. Step on the right foot to the right side.)
3. Verbalize "right" and "left" as it is performed.
4. Repeat the activity to the other side.

Learning Outcomes:
Students understand right and left in their own bodies, and can move to either side on cue.

Activity 4-20
bdpq
DIRECTIONALITY

Age:
3rd grade/older
Time:
3 minutes

Objectives:
To recognize rightness and leftness
from the view of another person
standing opposite the student.

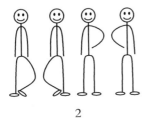

2

1. Students face their classmates.
2. Form alphabet letters with their bodies so they read correctly to observers.
   (example: Lower case b, d, p, q.)

Learning Outcomes:
Students recognize right and left sides of other people. This activity reinforces a
child's sense of directionality because the performer must reverse the direction
the letter is facing from the direction they would write it on paper.

Activity 4-21
CROSSING MIDLINES

Age:
K/3rd grade
Time:
1 minute

Objectives:
To cross sagittal, transverse, and frontal midlines of the body.

1. Stand tall with legs and arms spread apart.
2. Right arm crosses the body to touch the left foot.
3. Stand tall with legs and arms spread apart.
4. Repeat with the left hand to the right foot.
5. Swing the right leg forward and back and close next to the left.
6. Swing the left leg forward and back and close next to the right.

Learning Outcomes:
Students cross the sagittal (right and left sides of the body), transverse (upper and lower halves of the body), and frontal (front and back) midlines.

Sitting "criss-cross applesauce" (legs bent at knees and crossed one over the other in front) on the floor or giving oneself a big hug clutching knees to the chin also crosses midlines. (Students sitting on the floor forming a "w" shape with their legs are not crossing midlines.)

Activity 4-22
YARN BALL PASSING
CROSSING MIDLINES, DIRECTIONALITY, LATERALITY

Age:
3rd grade/older
Time:
3–5 minutes

Materials: Yarn balls (see Appendix A–3, page 171)
Objectives:
To reinforce crossing the midlines, directionality, and laterality.

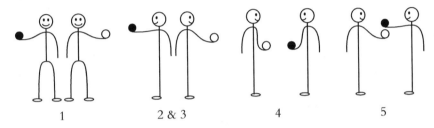

1   2 & 3   4   5

Use two different colored yarn balls: one color for the right, the other for the left.

1. Standing in a circle two students next to each other are each holding one of the balls.
2. The "right" ball student passes it to the right using only right hand, changing level of the ball, and changing direction (front or back) they are facing each time it is passed.
3. The "left" ball student does the same thing to the left.
   Then
4. When each ball has made it back to its original owner students form two lines facing each other.
   Then
5. Students, still changing levels with each exchange, pass the ball with the appropriate hand to the person across or diagonally across from them. (Ball is never passed back to the person who just had it.)

Learning Outcomes:
Students cross sagittal, transverse, and frontal midlines. Students also reinforce laterality and directionality.

**Kinesthetic
Sense**

Awareness of one's position and movement in space is perceived through nerve-end organs in muscles, tendons, and joints, and can be referred to as a kinesthetic sense of one's surroundings. A kinesthetic sense is not dependent on the aid of vision, which can be demonstrated, for example, by a blind person's ability to balance.

Activity 4-23
JUDGING DISTANCE

Age:
K/3rd grade
Time:
1 minute

Objectives:
To judge spatial distance and step size.

1. Place students around the room away from their desks or their belongings.
2. Count eight evenly spaced counts as students take eight same size steps to arrive back to their "home" place on the count of eight, not before it or after.

Learning Outcomes:
Students measure the spatial distance and step size needed to cross a specified area.

Activity 4-24

FOLLOW BUT DON'T BE FOLLOWED
KINESTHETIC SENSE

Age:
3rd grade/older
Time:
3–5 minutes

Objectives:
To reinforce a kinesthetic sense moving "in sync" and "out of sync" with others.

1. Within a larger designated open space, all students walk around the room using all the space, filling corners where there is no one else.
   Then
2. Gradually walk alongside someone else and try to move in sync with that person.
   Then
3. Gradually accelerate (but not run, with partner).
   Then
4. Decelerate (must keep moving), walking.
   Then
5. Moving alone (no partner), fill all the open spaces around the room.
   Then
6. Try to follow someone but do not let anyone else follow you.
   Then
7. Students walk alone again, gradually decelerate, and slowly come to a complete stop.

Learning Outcomes:

Students develop kinesthetic awareness by moving in sync with others, accelerating and decelerating in sync with others and trying to follow but not be followed.

Activity 4-25
BALANCE ON ONE LEG

Age:
K/3rd grade
Time:
1 minute

Objectives:
To strengthen kinesthetic sense. To center oneself and relax before moving on to a new activity.

1. Stand in personal space on both feet.
2. Place one leg in front of the other. Allow it to come a few inches off the floor and balance.
   Then
3. Close eyes and continue balancing on one leg. Think "very tall."
   Then
4. Lower the leg, and put both feet together.
   Then
5. Open eyes.
6. Repeat on the other side.

Learning Outcomes:
Students reaffirm kinesthetic awareness of their surroundings by balancing on one leg. They center themselves before moving on to another activity.

Using Props to Strengthen Kinesthetic Sense

Props or objects to be manipulated by students and teachers, as illustrated in the ball passing activity described earlier, enhance development of one's spatial and kinesthetic sense. Props are useful because they become extensions of body parts, form connections with other people, and define parameters of personal and general space.

The addition of balls, scarves and other hands-on objects including various size hula hoops provide many possibilities for strengthening both body awareness and spatial sensitivity (see Appendices A-2 and A-4).

Activity 4-26
WALKING TURTLES

Age:
Pre-K/K
Time:
3 minutes

Materials:
Hula hoops. This activity is best performed with five children per hoop. When available, "assistants" can hold additional hoops for groups of five children each. All groups can perform simultaneously.
Objectives:
To strengthen kinesthetic awareness, personal space, sense of direction, and body part identification.

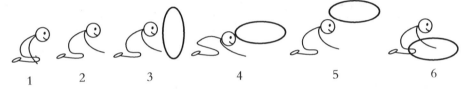

1   2   3   4   5   6

1. Students are turtles inside their shells. (example: Kneeling on the floor in personal space.)
   Then
2. Students identify their head, legs and arms coming out of and returning into their shell.
   Then
3. Teacher holds hula hoop perpendicular to the floor. (example: Turtles crawl through the tall grass.)
   Then
4. Hold the hoop parallel and close to the floor. (example: Turtles crawl over a rock.)
   Then
5. Raise the hoop higher. (example: Turtles crawl under a fallen branch.)
   Then
6. Place the hoop on the floor. (example: Turtles crawl around the pond, and then across the pond to take a nap in the sun.)

Learning Outcomes:
Students use different body parts, travel in different directions, and distinguish personal and general space.

Activity 4-27
PERSONAL SPACE ISLANDS

Age:
3rd grade/older
Time:
6–10 minutes

Materials:
Hula hoops
Objectives:
To define personal space and general space.
To judge distance. To work in sync with others.

1. Some students put themselves inside their hoop and, holding the hoop, move it up, above, and around their bodies to define and designate personal space.
2. Other students form a ring outside of and around the students with the hula hoops. They define and designate general space.
3. Hula hoop students, holding hoops in both hands, reach in all directions exploring personal space.
Then
4. Moving their personal space (with hula hoops) in all directions, they travel within the general space.
Then
5. On cue, the students forming the outside ring move in same sized steps synchronized with each other to gradually shrink the general space. Hula hoop students inside the circle adjust the size of their personal space accordingly.
Then
6. On cue, the outside ring of students moves in same sized steps synchronized with each other to gradually enlarge the general space.
Then
7. Students trade roles and repeat.

Learning Outcomes:
Students define personal space and change its size accordingly. Students work together judging distance to change the size of general space.

Activity 4-28
DANCING HULA HOOPS

Age:
3rd grade/older
Time:
10 minutes

Materials:
Hula hoops
Objectives:
To create group movements using a prop that affects the
movements.

1. Students are in groups. Each group has one hoop.
2. Each group member does something different with the hoop. (example:
   Twirl the hoop around their waists; leap over the hoop on the floor; jump
   through the hoop.)
   Then
3. Each group creates or selects five or six movements using the hoop
   as focal point.
   Then
4. Design their movements as one connected movement.
   Then
5. Perform their movement for the class without using the hoop.
   Then
6. Discuss differences in performing and observing the dance with and
   without the hoop. (examples: Did using the hoop help define spatial and personal relationships? Did students "see" the hoop when it was not being used?
   Was it easier or more difficult to perform without the hoop?)

Learning Outcomes:
Students create a dance based on using a particular prop and then perform the dance
itself without the prop. Working together they enhance their spatial and kinesthetic sense.

The preceding activities all focus on developing the physically moving body. Such
activity produces young people who are adept at and comfortable moving their
bodies through space and sharing that space with others. The physically moving self
is a significant part of every child, and a body that moves well immeasurably
enhances self-image.

> If a student is taught how to move his or her body, (to learn) what it is capable
> of doing, and that it is ok to try new, creative exercise forms at an early age, it
> can be a lifelong lesson.
>
> Fifth grade teacher

Notes for Chapter 4

1. National Association for Sport and Physical Education. (2004). *Moving into the Future: National Standards for Physical Education.* (2nd Edition). Reston, VA: NASPE. The National Association for Sport and Physical Education is part of the American Association of Health, Physical Education, Recreation, and Dance. www.aahperd.org.

2. Over the years there have been substantial research studies demonstrating that various forms of dancing can provide basic physical and cardiovascular fitness. Reviews of studies relating participation in dance activities to physical fitness are found in the Research in Dance Education database (www.ndeo.org/research). Go to "educational issue" category: health; and "area of service" category: dance science and medicine. Construction of this data base, by the National Dance Education Organization was one result of the research project cited in Note 1, Chapter 2.

3. See dance and arts education standards (K-4 and early childhood) noted earlier and listed in Appendix B-1, p. 175 and physical education standards, Note 1 above.

4. During the mid-to-late twentieth century researchers identified various groups of students who were experiencing learning difficulties in classroom settings. Coming from various fields of academia these theorists including Bryant Cratty, Carl Delacato, Marianne Frostig, Arnold Gesell, G. N. Getman, and Newell Kephart tried to determine if poor academic performance might have some physiological basis other than simply reflecting level of intelligence, laziness, or disinterest in a student's behavior. Such theories came under the heading of perceptual motor learning. For summaries of perceptual-motor learning theories see Lerch, et.al, *Perceptual-Motor Learning: Theory and Practice.*

5. Additional research regarding the significance of neural connections between moving and learning can be found in the Research in Dance Education database (www.ndeo.org/research). Go to "education issues" categories: kinesthetic learning; learning styles and theories; and/or brain research. Go to "areas of service" categories: child development, and/or cognitive development. Of particular interest is the 1990s research of physical educator, Marjorie Corso, that investigated possible correlations between body space and paper space used by elementary age students. Corso divided a piece of paper into three midlines to correlate with the midlines of the body: sagittal (right, left sides of the body), transverse (upper and lower parts of the body) and frontal (front and back). She then compared the children's use of body space in physical education activities and their use of paper space in the classroom. Her findings noted examples of children who did not cross the midline of their bodies or the midlines on paper. For example, some students who did not cross the midline dividing the upper and lower part of the body would draw only on the lower or upper half of the paper. Others not drawing on a particular quadrant of paper also might not use that body quadrant when moving (reaching only one arm in the air for example). Those not crossing the vertical (or sagittal) midline of the body when moving may not cross the vertical midline on paper or may change hands at the middle. Corso also found that these behaviors could be reflected in students' reading. Children who scrunched up their letters also had difficulty establishing personal space and might stand very close to others in line. Overall,

Corso found correlations between a child's coordination of arms and legs, the need for improvement in organizational skills, work habits, and/or disruptive behavior during activity transitions. For Corso's full four-part report see Corso, "Children Who Desperately Want to Read, but Are Not Working at Grade Level: Use Movement Patterns as "Windows" to Discover Why;" Part II: "The Transverse Midline;" Part III: "The Frontal Midline;" and Part IV: "Crossing All Three Midlines Automatically."

6. Dance educator Anne Green Gilbert has created a videotape titled *Brain Dance* which demonstrates movement and dance activities to reinforce neural connections. For availability, go to www.ndeo.org.

FIVE

Dancing as Kinesthetic Reinforcement of Learning

Something I particularly like about creative dance, that can be incorporated in my classroom, is the way that students of varying dance and academic levels can work together to learn and create something. Kinesthetically-gifted students who may not perform well in other academic disciplines may excel and learn about particular subject matter better when introduced and reinforced through movement.

Third grade teacher

How Do Students Learn?

Transmitting knowledge and sharing experience are goals of education. As facilitators of these objectives, teachers regularly question how students learn and try to identify strategies that appear to facilitate learning. Such moments occur when a particular student demonstrates difficulty with learning the subject at hand and teachers try different approaches. Often teachers of special education populations, for example, openly admit abandoning traditional teaching methods in pursuit of new ways to reach and teach an individual student. The reality is that, in most classrooms on a daily basis, teachers explore new paths to facilitate learning, often reflecting on their own experiences and how they learned.

How do students learn? Historically, this question was most often pursued by psychologists. Two opposing views surfaced in the mid-twentieth century: the behaviorist position associated with B. F. Skinner and the phenomenological point of reference attributed to Carl R. Rogers.[1]

Behaviorist Approach

The behaviorist view recognized people as relatively passive in behavior and governed by external stimuli. It claimed to be scientific, analytical, and objective.

*Fundamental sets of rules, standardized procedures, rote memorization of infor-
mation, and subordination to authority might effectively manage people's development and education.*

Identifying specific physical and psychological developmental stages children
pass through on their way to adulthood, education behaviorists thought they could
predict what, how, and when children learn. In this way they could standardize
appropriate achievement for specific ages of students, and measuring the success of
such achievement would produce accountability of education. However, observers
of human behavior like anthropologist Margaret Mead questioned the universality
of specified developmental stages in different populations of young people.[2]
Questions of standardization, accountability, and testing continue today as ongoing,
often polarizing, educational issues.

At the opposite end of the continuum from the behaviorist view, the
phenomenological approach was humanizing and subjective.

**Phenomenological
Approach**

*The phenomenological view placed people individually in control of their behav-
ior with freedom to make choices in different situations. Applying phenomenological philosophy to education involves students having an active say in their
learning process, making many choices in its implementation.*

The process of learning becomes just as significant, if not more so, than its
product, and the development of critical and creative thinking skills is nurtured.
Both approaches apply to dance activities. The behaviorist view is apparent when
learning traditional dances and dance movements, and it is important to replicate
the techniques of the original dance as closely as possible. However, when
originality and creativity are encouraged, the phenomenological or discovery
approach applies. Dance education easily employs both philosophical approaches
depending on the objectives of a specific lesson.

In 1983 Howard Gardner, a Harvard University psychologist, added new
insights to educational learning theory with the publication of his book, *Frames of
Mind: The Theory of Multiple Intelligences.*[3] The text was the result of more than two
decades of research identifying different faculties that people use to process information in a variety of situations. Participation in the arts was one of those situations.

**Theory of Multiple
Intelligences**

Providing alternative considerations of an intelligence model besides the traditionally applauded linguistic and logical mathematical intelligences, Gardner's work presented another possibility for answering questions about students and learning process. He proposed that there are seven intelligences: linguistic, logical-mathematical, spatial, musical, bodily-kinesthetic, interpersonal, and intrapersonal. He has since added an eighth intelligence: naturalist.[4] Gardner's work did not identify students with singular modes of learning. Rather, he believed that students may possess several intelligences and use them together or independently at different times. The introduction of Multiple Intelligence Theory motivated dance educators to demonstrate its potential application in dance activities by identifying the engagement of different intelligences during dance activity.

Using Eight Multiple Intelligences in Dance Activities

1. Students use **linguistic intelligence** when they use words to describe their dances and dance experience. They also employ it when creating dances from word sequences.

2. Students engage **logical–mathematical intelligence** when they count dance phrases, divide phrases into beats and movements, expand counts of phrases, and generally play with rearranging and designing movements according to numbers of counts.

3. Students draw on **spatial intelligence** when they shape their bodies to mold and reconfigure both personal and general space to form puzzle piece shapes, for example.

4. Students involve **musical intelligence** as they create rhythms with their movement, such as designing sound stories of a thunderstorm using their hands, voices, and feet.

5. Students use **bodily-kinesthetic intelligence** when they successfully control and isolate body parts in personal space and travel through general space with others.

6. Students engage **interpersonal intelligence** when they work together in groups communicating, cooperating, and understanding each other's ideas and feelings to create dances.

7. Students draw on **intrapersonal intelligence** when they develop a self-image recognizing their own strengths, likes, and dislikes as a result of creating dances.

8. Students involve **naturalist intelligence** when they move as different living things (animals, insects, plants), aspects of weather, or other natural things they observe and perceive around them.

Moving and Learning

During the closing decades of the twentieth century dance educators realized that recognition of students' different learning styles and attention to multiple intelligences could vitalize support for dance education in schools, since dancing activity could strengthen both objectives.

Interest in students' learning connected two different paths or trains of thought in dance education: dance as physical education and dance as arts education.

On one hand, students had been learning dance in physical education classes since the beginning of the twentieth century, and researchers had investigated relationships between motor development, physically moving, and learning achievement. On the other hand government and privately funded programs had supported dance as arts enrichment in public school programs during the latter half of the century. Those programs also stimulated research examining relationships between participation in arts activities and learning.[5]

This linking of paths in dance education was indicative of connections being forged across disciplines during the last half of the twentieth century. Dance education research discovered more and more examples of findings in cross-disciplinary exploration that supported learning occurring through dance, as well as in and about dance. Such examples of research represent disparate disciplines but suggest substantial earlier links between dancing and learning. A selected few follow:

Edward Seguin (1812-1880), French medical doctor, developed techniques for experiential learning utilizing movement and music. He believed that connections between sensory muscles and intellectual training must be made. His work focused on the education of mentally impaired children, but he alleged that such connections must be made for all young people. Maria Montessori credited Seguin's writing as an inspiration for her work.[6]

Rudolf Steiner (1861-1925), German philosopher, developed a movement practice called eurythmy that continues to be taught in Waldorf Schools today. Eurythmy has been described as visible speech because it makes visible the formative processes which are engaged before speech or music actually sounds. Educationally Steiner envisioned the study of eurythmy as enhancing the areas of language arts, arithmetic, music, and history.[7]

Emile Jaques-Dalcroze (1865-1950), Swiss composer and musician, realized the significance of children moving to experience music. Forced to resign from the Geneva Conservatory of Music for asking musicians to feel their music's rhythm by moving around the room, Dalcroze developed movement activities still in use today by music and classroom educators.[8]

Margaret Mead (1901-1978),[9] American anthropologist, studied dancing in Samoa as part of a child's educational and social development. In the 1950s, British anthropologist, John Blacking,[10] also correlated dancing with the cognitive development of children in Africa.

Sylvia Ashton-Warner (1908-1984), Australian elementary educator, chronicled her experience teaching Maori children in New Zealand using dancing, writing, and drawing as modes of expression.[11]

Harold Rugg (1886-1960), university educator, historian, and engineer, called for paralleling verbal education programs with non-verbal programs in *Imperatives for Education*. Rugg advocated creating not only a word-focused but also a motor-focused curriculum.[12]

These examples coming from diverse disciplines only reinforce what many individual teachers know from experience: that dancing activity engages students and learning reinforcement occurs. More and more educators are beginning to document these successes and conduct formal research to support further implementation of such activity.

Research journals from various disciplines along with federal and local government projects have published results of dancing in school experiments including application of dancing activity in reading, mathematics, social studies, and science classes.[13] Seven specific studies (four examining reading skills and three non-verbal reasoning skills) were discussed in *Critical Links: Learning in the Arts and Student Academic and Social Development* published by the United States Department of Education and The National Endowment for the Arts in 2002.[14]

Kinesthetic learning can be defined as "learning by doing," getting students up on their feet, and actively engaging them in learning by using other than traditional modes of reading, writing, and listening while sitting. Kinesthetic learning methodology appears to be popular with many students. In the 1990s Clara Park conducted a series of experiments investigating the learning style preferences of several thousand secondary school students from very diverse ethnic populations. The results determined that all populations tested indicated a strong preference for kinesthetic learning style.[15]

When dancing is used as kinesthetic learning, the emphasis is on the motivation for the moving, and what the moving represents.

To enhance the learning process, teachers can use the attributes of dance elements to strengthen/clarify details of the moving aspects of the subject, but participating students are not necessarily asked to think of the dance elements they may be applying or to think of the movement as dancing. Rather, they are encouraged to concentrate their thinking and understanding on the reason for, the subject of, the movement.

Learning Kinesthetically

Activity 5-1
TRIP FROM HERE TO THERE

Age:
3rd grade/older
Time: 20 minutes

Materials:
Paper and drawing
Objectives:
To reinforce map reading. To reinforce directions, pathways, and shapes. To create a map.

Introductory preparation:

Designate one side of the room as north. In this way, students can orient their maps to the space.

1. In groups, students draw a map on paper
   (one map produced from each group).
2. Locate HERE (starting point) and THERE (ending point),
   and North.
3. Connect HERE and THERE using different pathways.
   (examples: Curved, straight, zigzag.)
4. Draw several obstacles of different shapes on the way.
   (examples: Mountains, volcanoes, bodies of water, bridges, tunnels, forests or local items such as one-way roads, detours, railroad crossings.)
   Then
5. One group plots their map on the floor, forming the obstacles with their bodies.
   Then
6. Another group "reads" the paper map as they follow it and travel from HERE to THERE.
   Then
7. Groups reverse roles.

Learning Outcomes:

Students follow a map to arrive at a destination. They reinforce directions, pathways, and shapes as they learn how to read a map. They also express themselves non-verbally by creating a map for someone else to read.

Site and Lesson-Specific Map Reading Activities

Map reading assignments can

- Illustrate history lessons: tracking the Oregon Trail, crossing the United States, building the first railroad, or heading to the California Gold Rush.

- Explore aspects of earth science lessons: visiting a rain forest, a desert, or another unfamiliar terrain.

- Demonstrate biology lessons: traveling through the body's circulatory, skeletal, or digestive system.

- Enhance language arts lessons: following the trails of *Robinson Crusoe, The Little Prince,* or Homer's *Odyssey* (see Appendix A-22).

Applying attributes of the elements of dance provides contrasting movement experiences characteristic of the specific map trip.

- Select different parts of the body as students drive, walk, or use other locomotor transport.

- Travel different pathways and directions.

- Form contrasting shapes and vary levels used.

- Use changes in tempo and rhythm.

- Add syncopation within certain parts.

- Apply differing amounts of energy.

- Add music or appropriate sound effects to enhance time and energy attributes.

Map Reading Activities Can Engage Multiple Intelligences

- Employ linguistic intelligence by asking students to think of words to describe features of the terrain of their map.

- Use logical mathematical intelligence to plot the map to scale from the originally created map.

- Engage spatial intelligence by forming the shapes of obstacles with students' bodies and placing them in relation to each other.

- Utilize musical intelligence by providing sounds to identify the map's environment.

- Employ bodily-kinesthetic intelligence to move through (read) the map and relate to obstacles.

- Use interpersonal intelligence as students collaborate to create and agree on the map's final form.

- Engage intrapersonal intelligence when each student deals with compromising some of their ideas and realizes what is individually felt.

- Utilize naturalist intelligence by including aspects of natural surroundings, terrain, and living things specific to the area illustrated by the map.

Additional Examples for Kinesthetic Reinforcement of Learning Looking at the following activities, imagine how each could be further embellished, and learning reinforced, by using more attributes of dance elements and consciously engaging multiple intelligences. Involve students in discussion before, during, and following each activity to create multiple and contrasting possibilities. Stated time for each activity will vary depending on the number of students involved and length of discussion time.

Activity 5-2
BODY SPELLING★

Age:
K/3rd grade
Time:
10–12 minutes

Music:
Drum (see Appendix A–20, page 173)
Objectives:
To form concrete shapes of letters with the body. To compare movement qualities of writing in cursive with a hand alone and with a computer keyboard.

1   2   3   4 & 5

1. Form shapes of single letters with single body parts. (example: Letter "O" with arms.)
   Then
2. Form shapes of letters using the whole body. (example: Letter "T.")
   Then
3. Form letters with partners or groups. (example: Letter "A" with a partner. Letter "M" with three people.)
   Then
4. Select a word to body spell. (example: "CAT.")
   Then
5. Form each letter using the whole body.
   Then
6. Form each letter slowly and smoothly as if writing in cursive. (example: Count four slow beats for each letter. There is no stopping between letter formations.)
   Then
7. Form each letter quickly and suddenly as if writing on a computer. (example: Count one quick staccato beat for each letter. There is no visible moving into and out of the letter shape.)
   Then
8. Divide class into two groups. One group watches while the other group spells another word and tries to guess the word.
   Then
9. Groups reverse roles.

Learning Outcomes:
Students see many possibilities for forming the same letter. They experience variation in movement quality (writing in cursive versus writing with a computer).
★Activity 9-5 provides a full lesson plan developing variations of this activity.

Activity 5-3
OPPOSITES
ANTONYMS

Age:
K/3rd grade
Time:
3-5 minutes

Objectives:
To reinforce understanding of antonyms
and other opposites.

2

1. Students as partners select two words that are antonyms.
2. Illustrate the words using body shapes with partner. (example: One is "open,"
   the other is "closed.")

3

Then
3. Use counts as partners move from one shape to the other. (example: Use four
   counts to move from open to closed shapes. Partners move in opposition to
   each other.)
Then
4. Change the tempo (number of counts).
5. Vary amount of energy (strong or light, bound or free flow)
   for each movement.

Learning Outcomes:
Students kinesthetically experience opposites. They explore variations in timing

Activity 5-4
STATES OF MATTER
SOLID, LIQUID, GAS

Age:
3rd grade/older
Time:
5–10 minutes

Objectives:
To verbally describe movement qualities of matter.
To kinesthetically experience the differing qualities
of states of matter.

1. Verbally describe movement features of the states of matter: solid, liquid, gas.
   (example: Solid is firm, close, tight.)
   Then
2. Move as each state. Consider shape, tempo, and energy.
   Then
3. Change from one state to another.
   Then
4. Change tempo for transitions from one to another.
   Then
5. Change directions and levels of each movement.

Learning Outcomes:
Students kinesthetically experience features of states of matter.
They verbally describe movement qualities and variations.

Activity 5-5
GEOMETRIC SHAPES

Age:
All ages
Time:
5 minutes

Objectives:
To form concrete geometric shapes with the body.
To understand two-dimensional and three-dimensional geometric forms.

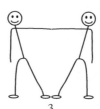

2   3

1. Create geometric shapes with individual body parts.
   (example: Form a diamond with legs.)
   Then
2. Create various sizes of the same shape with body parts.
   (example: Form a triangle with fingers, one leg.)
   Then
3. Repeat with partners and groups. (example: Use two bodies to form one
   triangle, use six bodies to form one.)
   Then
Older students
4. With partners or groups move from two-dimensional to three-dimensional
   shapes. (example: Form a flat two-dimensional triangle, move into a pyramid
   or three-dimensional form.)
5. Vary the speed of the changing shapes.
   Then
6. Select other shapes to form.

Learning Outcomes:
Students reinforce the forms of geometric shapes. They experience two- and
three-dimensional forms working with partners and groups.

Activity 5-6

MOVING MACHINES★

Age:
3rd grade/older
Time:
5-8 minutes

Objectives:
To introduce machines and their moving parts.
To understand repetitive movement.

1. Select different machines. Describe their movement features.
   (example: Washing machine fills with water, washes, and spins.)
2. Describe different parts that make up a machine such as levers, pulleys.
   (example: A pulley can raise a weight on one end by pulling on the other.)

Then

3. In groups students select a machine and demonstrate different working parts
   with their bodies. (example: Each person is a different part of the machine,
   performing a repetitive movement.)

Then

4. Students demonstrate their machines for each other and try to identify them.

Learning Outcomes:
Students experience repetitive movement. They are introduced to some
machines and their movement features. They expand both verbal and movement
vocabularies.

★Activity 9-8 provides a full lesson plan including a variation of this activity.

Activity 5-7
TRAVELING ON LAND, AIR, AND SEA

Age:
K/3rd grade
Time:
5–8 minutes

Objectives:
To introduce different forms of transportation and
to compare their movement features and qualities.

1. Identify ways to travel from one place to another including land, air,
   sea travel. (examples: Train, race car, mountain bike, glider, jet, helicopter,
   canoe, ocean liner.)
2. Describe pathways that each travel. (example: A mountain bike traveling a
   zigzag pathway.)
3. Describe tempo of each. (example: A jet traveling fast and in a straight line.)
4. Describe energy quality of each. (example: A glider moves slowly and
   indirectly.)
   Then
5. Using bodies contrast movements of different vehicles starting, traveling, and
   stopping in various settings. (example: In city traffic at rush hour, in a storm
   at sea, on a mountain trail in the snow, in the air on a sunny day.)

Learning Outcomes:
Students demonstrate and contrast different modes of transportation.
They experience variations in speed, energy, and pathways.

Dancing as kinesthetic reinforcement of learning challenges the thinking child to
create variations, to find alternative possibilities for solving a problem, and to engage
multiple intelligences. Using dance to kinesthetically reinforce learning focuses on
the academic subject to be learned, as determined by state academic subject area
content standards.

Notes for Chapter 5

1. Milhollan, *From Skinner to Rogers.*
2. Mead, "Coming of Age in Samoa."
3. Gardner, *Frames of Mind: The Theory of Multiple Intelligences.*
4. Gardner, *Intelligence Reframed: Multiple Intelligences for the 21st Century.*
5. For a review of dance education in elementary education during the twentieth century see Kraus, *History of the Dance in Art and Education,* pp. 292-342.
6. For further discussion regarding Seguin's application of experiential learning through movement see Dunkin-Willis, "The Integrative Aspects of Structured Movement Activity in the Education of the Whole Child: Contributions of Edward Seguin, Rudolf Steiner, Emile Jaques-Dalcroze, and Rudolf Laban."
7. Ibid.
8. Ibid.
9. See Note 2 above.
10. Blacking, "Movement, Dance, Music, and the Venda Girls' Initiation Cycle."
11. Ashton-Warner, *Teacher.*
12. Rugg, *Imagination.*
13. Reviews of such research are found in the Research in Dance Education database (www.ndeo.org/research). Search suggestions include "educational issue" categories: kinesthetic learning, student performance, student achievement, and/or interdisciplinary education. Also go to "service area" categories: pedagogy, child development, and/or cognitive development.
14. Arts Education Partnership, *Critical links: Learning in the Arts and Student Academic and Social Development.*
15. Park, "Learning Style Preferences of Korean-, Mexican-, Armenian-American and Anglo Students in Secondary Schools;" Park, "Learning Style Preferences of Asian American (Chinese, Korean, and Vietnamese) Students in Secondary Education;" Park, "Learning Style Preferences of Southeast Asian Students." Additional research studies documenting kinesthetic learning are found in the Research in Dance Education database cited above in Note 13. Go to "educational issue" category: kinesthetic learning.

SIX

Dancing as Cultural Play

*I like to dance with all the other kids. We get to perform in front of everybody
and that's really exciting to me.*

Student, nine years old

Dancing activity that involves actively looking, listening, thinking, moving, comparing, contrasting, reacting, and responding can be identified as cultural play.[1]

Broadly speaking, the term "cultural" refers to learned behavior; in other words, it
is knowledge that one gains through experience. [2]

School districts are composed of diverse populations, and within one school
there will be students representing many cultural backgrounds. Students enter
school with different pieces of knowledge forming their individual perceptions of
their surroundings and their position in those surroundings. Ultimately school
becomes a shared culture among students.

Play is part of this activity because dancing allows for momentary shifts or
flux (play) in the status quo in spatial and temporal relationships as well as in perceptions of oneself.

Notions of play involve the willing student, because play only exists when
and for as long as participants designate it.[3] Play exists when the participants have
a say in determining and enforcing the rules within parameters introduced by a
teacher/facilitator.

*As students are performing their dances, and (other) students are observing,
they are learning from each other. They are learning how to move, work
together, and most importantly they are learning to love dances from all over
the world.*

Third grade teacher

Roles Students Assume While Dancing

Young people engaging in cultural play while dancing have opportunities to
observe, to create, to perform, and to reflect and respond, not necessarily in that
order. Sometimes these occasions occur simultaneously and often spontaneously.
All provide learning opportunities.

Activity 6-1
BEING AN AUDIENCE
OBSERVING

Age:
K/3rd grade
Time:
Varies, depending
on presentation

Objectives:
To observe a live or filmed performance, make note
of specific features, and compare them with other
performances.

1. Encourage students to look and listen as they observe a performance.
2. Suggest specific features of the dance to describe. (example: What body parts,
    directions, and levels are used?)
3. Ask for a tabulation of one feature. (example: How many circles are in
    the dance?)
4. Suggest contemplation. (example: How does this dance make you feel?)

Learning Outcomes:
Students observe specific features that they can compare with other observations.
They observe others performing and can compare those performances with
their own.

Activity 6-2
CREATING DANCE ACTIVITIES

Age:
3rd grade/older
Time:
5 minutes

Objective:
To use creative thinking skills to create individual movement variations.

1. State a movement problem. (example: In sixteen counts, run quickly across the floor changing direction twice.)
   Then
2. Give students specific guidelines to follow in solving the problem. (example: In personal space, move three body parts lightly, then one part suddenly.)
   Then
3. As they become more comfortable, lessen the number of parameters given. (example: Create a series of light movements and stop suddenly.)
4. Use imagery. (example: Move like fireworks, exploding in all directions.)

Learning Outcome:
Students gain confidence in creating their own variations.

Activity 6-3
BEING A PERFORMER

Age:
All ages
Time:
Varies depending on
age and presentation

Objectives:
To feel comfortable performing for an audience. To
show dances to others.

1. Provide many short performance opportunities for students.
   (This helps them feel comfortable performing in front of others.)
2. Avoid the stress of one long-term heavily rehearsed presentation.
3. Encourage applause at the end of performances. (This shows respect for each
   other's work.)
4. For shorter spontaneous dances, applaud once after all groups have performed. (This eliminates competing to be the best or
   most popular.)

Learning Outcomes:
Students become comfortable moving their bodies as a form of expression and
performing for an audience. They learn to respect others' accomplishments.
They feel pride in performing their own creation.

Feeling comfortable when performing in front of others is important. Throughout
their lives, every time students attend a job or school interview or even meet someone new for the first time, they will be performing.

Activity 6-4
REFLECT AND RESPOND

Age:
All ages
Time:
Varies depending on
age and presentation

Objective:
To take time to reflect and respond about
the performance.

1. Ask students to reflect on things that they especially liked.
   (example: Identify similar and dissimilar attributes
   of dance elements.)
2. Discuss individual interpretations and feelings about the dance.
   (example: Did you like the straight line dance or
   the circle dance best?)
3. Challenge students to elaborate on their choices.
   (example: Why do you prefer one over another?)
   Note the validity of each group of responses. (example: Isn't it interesting that
   some like circle dances, while others prefer straight line dances?)
4. Use written essays or group discussion to explore how students
   felt about each dance.
5. Use written reflection or one-on-one discussion to respond
   to individual performances.

Learning Outcomes:
Students discuss their individual feelings and their performance of the activity.
They learn there are different, equally valid interpretations for the
same performance.

Encouraging students to become active observers, creators, performers, reflectors and
respondents involves thinking critically.

The Element of Choice as Cultural Play

Encouraging creativity involves providing opportunities for students to make
choices, to discover alternative solutions to situations rather than looking for a single right or wrong answer.

Activity 6-5
DIFFERENT CHOICES

Age:
All ages
Time:
3–5 minutes

Objectives:
To make individual choices and recognize their validity.

1. Place pre-schoolers on their stomachs forming baskets by holding their ankles in their hands behind them.
   Then
2. Go to each student and ask each one what is in their basket. (example: Eggs, candy, dolls, pineapple.)
3. Encourage students to keep thinking of different items.

Or

4. Place first graders in personal space.
   Then
5. Ask them to discover how many triangles they can form with different body parts at the same time.

Or

6. Place third graders in partners.
   Then
7. Ask them to find different ways to travel across the floor without using their feet.

Or

8. Place fifth graders in small groups.
   Then
9. Ask them to create an eight count movement phrase.
   Then
10. Have them choose two totally different ways to perform it.

Learning Outcomes:
Students learn they can make acceptable choices that are not necessarily the same as their neighbors. They learn that there is not one right answer.

**Social, Cultural,
Artistic Choices**

When treating dance as cultural play, there are social, cultural, and artistic choices which are not totally independent of each other. They will most likely overlap and intersect with one another.

Social choices made while moving within a dancing activity may include where or next to whom to place oneself, whom (if anyone) to copy, and what role to assume alongside others. Social choices exist in the present, and they reflect immediate desires to belong to, to be accepted by, and to participate as group member.[4] Social choices may be most evident in spatial positions chosen by participants.

Cultural choices made during a dancing activity may appear in verbal communication and familiar gestures and moves. They may also involve how much space is used, at what tempo tasks are pursued, and how much energy is expended in the process. Cultural choices may reflect individual heritage, such as place of birth and primary written and spoken language. They may mirror the specific school culture regarding accepted codes of behavior. They may also echo popular culture choices of clothing, music, and performing artists.

Artistic choices during dancing activity involve concern for the form of the dance, the quality of its presentation, recognition that there may be more than one way—sometimes even better ways—to design the movement, and how each way is chosen. Artistic expressions engage a student as both creator and as craftsperson. Students emerge as craftspeople by developing skills through repeated artistic choices over time.

**Leading and
Following**

As students create and pursue dance expression, they assume and often interchange roles as leaders and followers. Variations of leading and following strategies are further identified as **shadowing, mirroring, echoing,** and **call and response.** These four approaches can provide the focus of a lesson plan.

Shadowing places the student (or follower) directly behind the teacher (or leader).

Shadowing is a good teaching technique for beginning students since all movements for each participant occur on the same side of the body, and thus there is no confusion about right and left sides. Shadowing also refers to placing oneself in close proximity to another and following, or copying his/her every move.

Students who do not wish to be seen clearly or to take the initiative for leading usually choose to shadow, often placing themselves directly behind their classmates.

Activity 6-6
SHADOWING

Age:
K/3rd grade
Time:
3-5 minutes

Objectives:
To follow behind the leader and copy every move.

1. Place students in partners.
   Then
2. Each partnership decides who will be #1 and #2.
   Then
3. #1 (the first leader of the two) moves across the room writing his/her name on an imaginary piece of paper that extends from the ceiling to the floor. Use many different body parts and levels. Cover as much of the "paper" as possible.
4. #2 (the follower) shadows the movement following close behind.
   Then
5. Repeat with #2 as leader and #1 as the shadow.

Learning Outcomes:
Students concentrate and try to exactly replicate movements.

Mirroring places the teacher (or leader) in front of the student (or follower), facing them.

This is often a desired technique for teaching dance sequences because the teacher or leader faces the students, moves to the same side with them, and can monitor their behavior. Of course, while mirroring, teachers or leaders actually move in opposition to the students or followers (if students move to their right side, teachers or leaders will be moving to their left side).

Activity 6-7
MIRRORING

Age:
K/3rd grade
Time:
3–5 minutes

Objectives:
To concentrate on partner's movements and try to copy his or her movements simultaneously using directionality.

1. Partners designate #1 and #2.
2. Partners face each other and practice mirroring.
   #1 is the person looking in the mirror and initiating the movement.
   #2 is the mirror and simultaneously reflects #1's movement.
   Then
3. Repeat with #2 initiating movement, and #1 reflecting it.
   Then
4. Tell a story in movement, move around the room, or whatever the initiator chooses.

Mirroring Variation 1
Age: K/3rd grade
Time: 3 to 5 minutes

1. Movement initiator tries to surprise reflection by moving suddenly and unexpectedly and making simultaneous reflection impossible.

Mirroring Variation 2
Age: 3rd grade/older
Time: 5 minutes

1. Divide class into audience and performing couples.
   Then
2. Audience closes their eyes for a few moments to allow mirroring partners to begin moving together.
3. The mirroring partners practice fooling the observers about who is leading and who is following. (This requires total concentration and working together.)
   Then
4. When audience opens its eyes, see how soon they can guess who of the mirroring partners is leading the movement.

Learning Outcomes:
Students concentrate and closely observe. They work together with their partners to fool the audience.

Students may choose to mirror actions of other classmates for a variety of reasons. They may like the movement and want to try it out themselves. They may think it is better than something they can think of on their own. Or they may simply wish to work with that person. Although they are not taking the initiative to begin the movement, they are not trying to hide as the shadowing student may be.

Echoing occurs when students (or followers) replicate the teacher's (or leader's) movement after it has taken place.

This is the third leading technique, and it is a variation of mirroring and shadowing. Teachers demonstrate or provide an example, and students replicate the movement after it was performed. Unlike shadowing and mirroring when the movement occurs simultaneously, echoing occurs after the model. This necessitates that followers pay close attention, remember, and then try to repeat exactly the desired activity. Some students feel more secure with this type of instruction, and develop proficient skill at becoming accomplished echoes in all classroom activities.

Activity 6-8
ECHOING

Age:
3rd grade/older
Time:
3–5 minutes

Objectives:
To concentrate, observe and repeat actions accurately after they have occurred.

1. Partners designate #1 and #2. #1 is the "voice"
   (the original movement) and #2 will "echo" the movement.
Then
2. #1 moves any way he or she wants to for four counts.
Then
3. #2 echoes the four counts of movement.
Then
4. #2 becomes the voice and #1 becomes the echo.

Learning Outcomes:
Students reinforce concentration, observation, and memory skills.

Call and response asks the student (or follower) to respond in their own way to the teacher's (or leader's) movement.

This leading technique is desired for creative dancing activities--because students create their own answers. It resembles a conversation with each party "listening" (not moving) and then "answering" (moving). The initiating movement is not repeated unless the respondent chooses to answer in that way. When repetition does occur, it is not an exact but rather a variation of the earlier movement.

Activity 6-9
CALL AND RESPONSE

Age:
3rd grade/older
Time:
3–5 minutes

Objectives:
To concentrate and know when to respond. To create differing responses.

1. Partners designate #1 and #2.
   Then
2. #1 begins a movement conversation by creating four counts of any movement.
   Then
3. #2 responds by creating four counts of other movement.
   Then
4. The two go back and forth allowing each to move for four counts before the other responds.
5. Students try "to tell" different stories.

Learning Outcomes:
Students concentrate, focus, and conduct a movement conversation with others.

Although call and response is a good technique for creative dancing activities, some students may be resistant at first, and may not be able to handle the freedom that call and response encourages. They will need time to feel more comfortable, and they may prefer participating in shadowing, mirroring, and echoing activities first.

Activity 6-10
LEADING AND FOLLOWING

Age:
All ages
Time:
3–5 minutes

Objectives:
To develop leading and following skills.
To create choices.

1. Discuss leading and following positions and choices with students.
   (example: These may be observable behaviors on the playground or in class; they may appear in traditional dances; they may be utilized in creative dance activities.)
   Then
2. Place students in partners. Assign #1 and #2.
   Then
3. Take turns leading and following. #1 leads the movement first,
   #2 follows.
   Then
4. Change roles.
   Then
5. Discuss which role students preferred and why.

Learning Outcomes:
Students discover their preference for leading or following. They acknowledge both and understand the appropriate time and place for each.

Developing leading and following skills, as part of group cultural play, is quite evident in students' dance choices absorbed from popular culture. Twenty-first century popular culture dancing includes hip hop, Latin, and ballroom dances. All of these incorporate a sense of style, attitude, and attention to dress. Students' participation in these dances illustrates their "trying on" and experimenting with new identities as they join others and build social relationships. Once students have learned a few basic steps and postures, they are free to create their own variations and new steps. With hip hop especially, individual interpretations and attitudes are not only encouraged but expected.

Activity 6-11
HIP HOP

Age:
3rd grade/older
Time:
20 minutes

Music:
Provided by students
Objectives:
To create a dance using hip hop style.

Introductory Information:
Hip hop had its beginning with break dancing in the 1970s. Originally, b-boys and b-girls got their name because they danced during the breaks in the music played by a DJ. Accompanied by their boom boxes, they soon began performing on street corners in New York and Los Angeles. These young people, predominately male African-American and Hispanic youth from lower income neighborhoods, created their own moves, driven by the music's rhythm and often inspired by media images such as Steve Martin's "robot," and Michael Jackson's "moon walk." As break dancing grew in popularity, dance crews "battled" (competed with) other crews to see who could create the most innovative and daring moves.

Rap music, graffiti, specific attire, and dancing all became expressions of hip hop culture as the participating young people found expressive outlets and a new sense of direction for their daily lives. The dances followed a certain format with individual dancers entering the ring of observers and trying to outdo the previous dancer. Performing in personal space and using multiple body parts, the dancers usually incorporated quick, sharp familiar movements such as punching, thrusting, pulling, and stomping. Dances ended with a signature pose (see Appendix A-5).

Activity 6-11, continued

Students in personal space perform the following:

Part A (24 counts)

1. Bending knees, walk forward four steps. Thrust alternating arms as if punching.
   Then
2. Bending knees, walk backward four steps. Bend alternating arms as if pulling in.
   Then
3. To right side step, step together, step, stomp and clap.
   Then
4. Repeat on left side.
   Then
5. Thrust right leg to right side and stomp on foot.
6. Thrust left leg to left side and stomp on foot.
7. Thrust right arm up 45 degrees above right shoulder.
8. Thrust left arm up 45 degrees above left shoulder.
   Then
9. Bend left arm at elbow, placing left hand on left shoulder.
10. Lean head on right arm, and thrust weight into right hip.
    Then
11. Drop both arms to sides of body, pull both legs together.
12. Lift right knee in front of body, pull arms close to chest.
    Then
13. Perform movements again with individual interpretation and attitude.

Part B (32 counts)

1. Students repeat Part A and add their own moves for seven counts and finish with a signature pose. (example: Any posture that a student chooses to represent his or her persona. "Macho" poses were popular in the 1970s.)
   Then
2. Divide class into two groups. Each group performs 32 counts for the other. Group members perform their own dances, simultaneously with their other group members.
   Then
3. Discuss the influence of contemporary television, motion picture and advertising images on hip hop dance.
4. Students create and demonstrate new hip hop moves using media images as inspiration.
   Then
5. Students discuss the impact of cultural choices on dance and arts expressions. They describe their dances using the elements of dance and their attributes.

Activity 6-11, continued

Learning Outcomes:
Students create variations for a popular dance style. They understand sources for popular dance forms. They work alone and together in groups. They compare each other's dances and appreciate their creativity. They use the elements of dance and their attributes to describe the dances, and as a result contrast the significance of space attributes versus parts of the body attributes versus time attributes and energy attributes

---

Besides hip hop dancing, the movies of the 1990s and turn of the twenty-first century sparked new interest for all ages in ballroom dancing including Latin dances.[5] The film *Mad Hot Ballroom*,[6] produced in 2005, chronicles the experiences of fifth grade students from sixty New York City elementary schools learning ballroom dancing which included the foxtrot, rumba, meringue, and tango to compete in an annual tournament. Participation in all of these dance forms engages students in cultural play as they experience the style, attitude, posture, and attire associated with each. Most of these dances can be performed as solos or in couples. Viewing and/or learning these dances inspired by popular culture can be included as part of dance education at school (see Appendix A-6).

Identity, Self-Esteem, and the Willing Child

When students explore and actively assume roles as leaders or followers within dance activities, they may discover different perceptions of their own and each other's identities. For example, a shy and quiet student may contribute creatively to the group, or an aggressive student may become an intent follower. As students successfully perform and gain respect for their expressions, they may want to push further. Expending effort, trying to do one's best, and subsequently creating something that did not exist before, individually or as a group, produces a sense of accomplishment--an important reward for students' self-esteem. And most importantly, students become willing participants in future activities.

I like the moves I make up. I think it's fun when you're trying so hard to do something.

Student, twelve years old

Notes for Chapter 6

1. For a theory of young people dancing as cultural play see Dunkin-Willis, "Marking Time and Space Together: An Interpretation of Young People's Dancing as Cultural Play."

2. For suggestions that individuals learn behavior from many communities see Rosaldo, *Culture and Truth: The Remaking of Social Analysis.*

3. For theoretical concepts defining and determining the presence of play see Huizinga, *Homo Ludens: A Study of the Play Element in Culture;* Bateson, "A Theory of Play and Fantasy;" and Caillois, *Man, Play, and Games.*

4. Anthropologist Victor Turner developed theories of communitas and social drama. See Turner, *The Ritual Process: Structure and Anti-structure.*

5. See Large, "The Next Dance." This newspaper article dated July 17, 2005, echoes other media reports describing a renewed interest in ballroom dance in the United States. Author cites the PBS program "Championship Ballroom Dancing" and motion pictures such as *Saturday Night Fever, Scent of a Woman, Strictly Ballroom,* and *Shall We Dance* as sparking the interest.

6. The documentary film, *Mad Hot Ballroom.* Written and co-produced by Amy Sewell, co-produced and directed by Marilyn Agrelo. Distributed by Paramount Classics, 2005.

SEVEN

Dancing as Arts Education

I like to dance because it is a way to express
yourself in creative ways and it is fun to learn.
Student, 10 years old

Dancing as arts education presents dancing as an art-making process along with music, theater, and visual arts. It introduces dance as its own subject matter with a history, a variety of practices, and specific structural attributes. Activities use dance vocabulary and dance-specific analysis. Such consideration fulfills specific content and achievement standards for pre-K through elementary school dance education (see Appendix B-1).

Dance as arts education engages the feeling child because arts activities involve the expression, interpretation, and reflection of feelings for both the participants and the audience. It provides benefits to learning not necessarily associated with dancing as physical education, kinesthetic reinforcement of curriculum, and cultural play.

Objectives for Dance as Arts Education[1]

- To encourage individual expression and creativity.

- To provide opportunity to take risks and approach activities in different ways.

- To develop sensitivity for the form and craft employed in expressions.

- To appreciate diversity in expression and aesthetic viewpoints.

- To foster understanding of cultural diversity: different people, places, times.

Studying dance as an art form involves first identifying the activity as dance, and then using the language of the dance elements–body, space, time, and energy–to create dances, to describe dances, and to analyze them. Earlier our discussions involved answering such questions as what parts of the body or bodies are accentuated? What body shapes, levels, and group configurations are formed? On what pathways and in what directions are the bodies moving in space? How long does the dance or parts of it last? Is it fast or slow? What rhythmic elements are present? What type of and how much energy is engaged?

Dance as an Art Form

Now we also consider the communication of the dance and dancers, feelings expressed by the performance, and interpretations of the dancers and the audience.

For example, questions about the dance might include the following:

- How do the dancers relate to each other? Why do you think this?

- What do you think the dancers are trying to show in their dancing?

- What do you think the choreographer wanted to express?

- How does performing (or watching) the dance make you feel?

- Did the dancers perform in general or personal space? What does this say to you?

- What parts of the body are accentuated? What words would you use to describe their movements?

- Did you notice repetitions in the movement? Describe what you saw.

- Does the tempo or energy change? How did those changes make you feel?

- Why do you think the choreographer made those choices?

Discussing dance as an art form involves considering the form used and choices made in individual creativity and expression. Recognize the possibility of many interpretations of one expression. Appreciate and respect the diversity that individual self-expressions produce. Take time to actively reflect on the dancing: note and celebrate the variety of expressions that students create solving the same movement

Individual Creative Expression:
Taking Risks and Finding Different Approaches

assignment. Encourage students to take risks, to dare trying movements different from what they or their classmates have done before, as they actively explore possible forms their dance may take.

**Sensitivity
for Form**

The notion of form suggests several applications. First, the form may be designated by a specific style of dance. Second, the form may be defined by its source of inspiration, whether it is story- or movement-inspired. Finally, attention to the quality of the dance's final form, when it is presented, is important. All three aspects of form are reflected in the craft that choreographers or dance makers develop over time.

Recognition of specific styles of movement. Dance styles such as ballet, modern, tap, or hip hop may define a dance's form. Developing performing skills in differing dance styles like these may be beyond the realm of dance in school settings. However, students are familiar with different dance styles, and showing video or films of them to stimulate discussions about their similarities and differences is part of arts education at school. All styles of dance use attributes of the elements of dance.

Story-inspired and movement-inspired forms. Throughout the history of dance there have been times when choreographers or dance makers wanted to tell stories with their dances, and other times when they chose to explore the possibilities of movement. Both are valid sources for inspiration, and both utilize parts of the elements of dance as the following examples illustrate:

Activity 7-1
MOVEMENT FORM
CHANGING LEVELS

Age:
K/3rd grade
Time:
1 to 2 minutes

Objectives:
To perform movement and concentrate on the movement itself. To use three levels of the body.

1. Students stand in columns on one side of the room.
2. First row, bodies and arms rise to high level.
   Then
3. Bodies drop to low level.
   Then
4. Students run middle level across the floor.
   Then
5. Repeat with each row of students.

Learning Outcomes:
Students reinforce levels of the body. They concentrate on performing movement exactly the way it is described.

Activity 7-2
STORY FORM

Age:
K/3rd grade
Time:
1 to 2 minutes

Objective:
To tell a story with movement.

1. Students stand in columns on one side of the room.
2. First row, each becomes a balloon and rises high in the air.
   Then
3. Balloons hit a sharp object, pop, and fall to the floor.
   Then
4. A broom sweeps them quickly across the floor.
   Then
5. Repeat with each row of students.

Activity 7-2, continued
Learning Outcomes:
Students concentrate on the story element itself rather than the movement.
They observe different interpretations in the movement performances of
their classmates.

The first example above is movement-driven and the second is story-inspired. Both use the whole body and the same levels and directions in space, but they differ in the timing and the amounts of energy presented in the descriptions. Both can be described by the elements of dance, but each is different in the form it takes and consequently the feeling it may evoke for participants and observers.

Reinforcing student effort. Most students strive to perform their best when presenting their own creations. A primary objective for offering dancing in pre-school and elementary school arts education is to reinforce creating, perform-ing, and recognizing one's best effort. Additionally, attention to details of perform-ance or final form can carry over to preparation of other class assignments, where creative choices will be made, and to overall neatness of assignments.

**Appreciating
Diversity in
Dance Expression
and Aesthetic
Viewpoint**

Dance activities can both connect with history lessons and recognize the diversity in expression and aesthetic feelings of different dance forms. The follow-ing two contrasting forms derive from European court dances, a precursor of clas-sical ballet, and rhythm-driven dances that are similar to step, clog, and tap dance forms today. The two activities, incorporating dance history, are designed for upper elementary-age students.

Activity 7-3
17TH CENTURY WALKING DANCE
(*PAVANE*)
LARGE SPACE DANCES

Age:
4th grade/older
Time:
30 minutes

Materials:
Paper and drawing utensils, portraits of
seventeenth- eighteenth-century European royalty, and
dance notation information (see Appendix A-7, page 171)
Music:
Pavane music
Objectives:
To explore the historical and aesthetic significance in the
movements of a seventeenth-century dance. To introduce a
method for recording dances.

Introductory Information:

Classical ballet originated in the Italian and French Courts of the late sixteenth/
early seventeenth-centuries. Its aesthetic and style reflected the movements of
early court dances that emphasized proud vertical alignment of the body, desire
to display one's presence at its best angles, traveling in symmetrical pathways, and
forming geometric configurations. These were important sensitivities of that
time and place. Tall, attractively positioned moving bodies reflected power, and
visible symmetry connoted a sense of order. Within that environment the *Pavane*
(also *Pavan*), a slow processional walking dance, performed by couples advancing and retreating, was popular.

1. Students study portraits of seventeenth- and eighteenth-century European
   royalty. (example: Describe attire. Consider dancing in that attire. Discuss
   one's behavior when meeting royalty, and how it might feel to be introduced
   at court.)
   Then
2. Students define associated vocabulary. (example: Symmetry, order, verticality,
   power, proud, and the name *Pavane* from the Latin word *pavo* meaning
   peacock.)
3. Students demonstrate definitions of these words using movement.
   Then
4. Discuss dancing manuals. (example: Invention of printing press made distribu-
   tion possible. Early manuals illustrate dances by showing pathways and spatial
   configurations.)

Activity 7-3, continued

Then

5. Students demonstrate straight, curved, zigzag, and symmetrical pathways by walking, walking on the balls of their feet, and walking with bent knees.

Then

6. Students form groups to create their own dances.

7. Each group draws a floor pathway on paper of symmetrical, geometric shaped configurations.

Then

8. In general space they follow the designed pathway performing a slow walking dance. (example: Using different pathways and directions, changing levels of the body, using light and sustained energy for 64 counts or one minute duration.)

Then

Begin here

9. Perform the dance for class to Pavane music from a Renaissance music collection. (example: Imagine they are appropriately attired, performing at court, and meeting royalty.)

Then

10. Students reflect on the performances.

11. They discuss how the dances "felt." (example: When they were dancing AND when they were observing, what words would they use to describe the feeling of the dance?)

12. They discuss the dances' structures. (example: What geometric configurations did they see/use? How many times did they see/use symmetrical movement? What levels of the body were used? Describe the energy used and the tempo of the dance. How important was a large space for this dance?)

13. They compare their Pavanes with classical ballet performances.[2] (example: Relate symmetrical movement and geometric configurations to the movements of the *corps de ballet*. Relate symmetrical, curved movement to the *port de bras* (arm movements) of ballet dancers. Relate a tall, vertical line in the body to a ballerina dancing on point.)

14. They think of words to describe the movements in classical ballet performances. (example: Fluid, graceful, smooth, harmonious, symmetrical, beautiful, orderly.)

Learning Outcomes: Students develop an aesthetic sense of classical ballet and its precursors by studying an early dance. Students develop an understanding for dances that utilize larger spaces as they reinforce their use of directions, pathways, and shapes. They expand movement and verbal vocabularies by describing the movements using the elements of dance and their attributes.

Contrast the style and aesthetic feeling of the *Pavane* with rhythm-driven dances. In the United States, rhythm-driven dances were created in spaces such as the slave quarters of eighteenth- and nineteenth-century plantations in the south and the street corners of crowded immigrant neighborhoods in large cities like New York and Chicago.

Activity 7-4
RHYTHM STORIES
RHYTHM-DRIVEN DANCES

Age:
3rd grade/older
Time:
25 minutes

Objectives:
To introduce dances based on individually created rhythms.

Introductory Information:
Historically, rhythm-driven dances expressed individual feelings, mimicked familiar sounds, and exchanged stories through rhythms created by sounds of feet, hands, and voices. Some of these dances today include step, clog, and tap dancing. Appreciating rhythm-driven dances involves listening to their sounds, noting the preciseness of their rhythms, and identifying the story they may be telling.

1. Students discuss telling stories using their hands, feet, and voices.
2. They identify the rhythms (patterning of accented and unaccented beats) that they hear every day and what those rhythms may be communicating. (example: The tick-tock of a clock is accented, the whirr of an engine is unaccented.)
3. They consider rhythm as an underlying attribute for dance expression. (example: Consider both the dance structure and communication between dancers.)
4. They discuss music they like, and relate the music's rhythm to their appreciation of the dance.
   Then
5. Place students in groups to create their own rhythm stories. (example: Use sound and movement of feet, hands, and voices—all three must be used. Use personal or general space. Story lasts 64 counts or one minute.)
6. Use one of the following scenarios:
   Thunderstorm. Slow drizzle accelerates to heavy fast rain, thunder/lightning.
   Cuckoo clock. Ticking hour, minute, and second hands.

Activity 7-4, continued

> *Steam engine train.* Clickety-clack metallic sound of train wheels against the track, traveling very fast, then slowing down, pulling into station, stops. *Galloping horses.* Traveling fast. Hear in the distance, they pass by, continue off into the distance. Tempo does not change.

Then

7. Students perform their Rhythm Stories for the class.

Then

8. Students discuss their dances.

9. They discuss how the dances "felt." (example: When they were dancing and when they were observing, what words would they use to describe the feeling of the dance?)

10. They discuss the structures of the dances. (example: How important was space in their dances? They compare differences in the tempo and rhythm of each dance and the energy each used.)

11. They compare their Rhythm Stories to other dance forms.[3] (examples: Step, clog, and tap dance. What words would they use to describe each?)

12. They imagine other subjects for Rhythm Stories dances. (example: What might the feelings and stories of dancers in the slave quarters and on crowded street corners have been?)

Learning Outcomes:

Students create group dances to tell a story using rhythms they create with their hands, feet, and voices. They compare these to other dance forms that accentuate the dance element of time and its attributes. They develop an understanding of when and how these dances might be created.

Both dance experiences above provide good opportunities for students to describe their movements in terms of the elements of dance because the *Pavane* and Rhythm Stories emphasize contrasting attributes of each element. They demonstrate differing dance forms and subsequent aesthetic feelings evoked in the participants and the audience as well. Contrasting these dances nurtures appreciation for diversity.

What is especially important about both of these activities is the reflection asked of the students while planning, performing, and discussing their dances qualitatively.

As part of this process students recognize dance as its own subject. They begin to understand that it has a diverse history and that individual dances have form and structure. They also consider how a dance "feels:" how the structure of the dance affects its feeling, how students feel performing it, and how their dance communicates those feelings. Such analysis fulfills specific content and achievement standards for dance education (see Appendix B–1).

Dance content and achievement standards also require that students understand dance in various cultures. Throughout its history dance, as expressions of people's feelings and ideas, has served several, often overlapping, functions.

Fostering Understanding of Cultural Diversity: Different People, Places, Times

These may include celebrating an event, telling a story, asking for something, promoting group solidarity and membership, maintaining ritual tradition, and recreation. Many of these dances have religious or ritual significance, so it is important to instill in students respect for these dances and what they mean to the people who created them.[4]

A few examples of dances that are accessible for school use and that illustrate variety in their function and structure appear in Activity 7-5. These specific dances from different times and places all utilize the elements of dance in contrasting ways. Students can study these dances by looking at a video, seeing a performance of them,[5] and/or actually learning them in school.

Activity 7-5
DANCES OF DIFFERENT PEOPLE, PLACES, TIMES

Age:
(See specific dance)
Time:
10–20 minutes
depending on age

Materials:
World map, video/DVD/CD (see Appendix A-8, page 172)
Objectives:
To introduce a dance from another time and place to students. To identify the dance's geographical location, its history and significance to the people who created it, and describe their apparel when dancing. To create variations of the dance.

Bongo (K/3rd grade) and **Highlife** (3rd grade/older)
These two West African dances performed to drum accompaniment demonstrate the improvisational nature of many African dances and might be described as recreational call and response games. Participants stand in a circle, and the leader in the center of the circle creates movements different from movements previous leaders have performed (see Appendix A-9).

Bongo and **Highlife Variations**
Students in a circle improvise a call and response dance in which the leader (in the center) creates a movement and rhythm and the others answer with a new *movement* and *rhythm.*

Chicken Dance (Pre-K/K)
Originally called "Duck Dance," this dance, which may have originated in Germany, is performed at weddings, during *October Fest,* and other social celebrations. Dancers open and close fingers like beaks, fold arms like flapping wings, and shake hips like tail feathers (see Appendix A-10).

Chicken Dance Variation
Students think of other animals in the barnyard, zoo, or other animal habitat. They create three different *body part movements* for each animal and then replace the three movements in the dance with those of the new animal.

Haka (3rd grade/older)
This New Zealand Maori dance asks for unity, spirit, and strength as participants prepare for battle. Performed without accompaniment other than the participants' chanting, this dance uses strong motions to illustrate positions of power and use of different hand held weapons (see Appendix A-11).

Activity 7-5, continued
Haka Variation
Students create a pre-sports game rallying cheer emphasizing *strong* movement to reinforce group unity and to garner strength and spirit to go with a particular athletic sport they are about to play.

Hora (3rd grade/older)
Meaning circle, this is a national dance of Israel and supports group solidarity. Traditionally dancers place their arms on each other's shoulders, and travel in a closed circle moving to the left or clockwise. Variations utilize a grapevine step (see Appendix A-12).

Hora Variation
Students create a unison group circle dance, holding hands or holding onto each others shoulders, that incorporates changes in *tempo*.

Huayno (K/3rd grade)
The Andean Mountains in South America is home for this festival dance. Composed of small running steps, the dance is performed in partners, circles, or lines. An interesting variation is a follow the leader version when dancers place hands on waists or shoulders of the person in front of them and follow serpentine pathways (see Appendix A-13).

Huayno Variation
Students create a unison dance moving in *different curved pathways*. The leader, who determines the direction, changes often.

Hukilau (3rd grade/older) and Aloha Kakahiaka (K/3rd grade)
These dances from Hawaii demonstrate the use of arm and hand movements to tell stories. They describe daily activities and natural surroundings such as going fishing, swimming, feasting, swaying palm trees, volcanoes, and the sun rising. The lower body sways side to side like the movement of ocean waves as feet follow a step-together-step pattern (see Appendix A-14).

Hukilau and Aloha Kakahiaka Variations
Students select their own scenario regarding daily life and surroundings in Hawaii (or a country of choice) and tell it through a dance of their *arms*.

La Raspa (Pre-K/K)
Very popular at *Cinco de Mayo* celebrations, this Mexican dance incorporates the "bleking" step (heel, heel, heel, clap, clap) found in European folk dances. It may be performed by couples or in a circle. The title, meaning a rasp or iron file, refers to the sound the dancers' feet make on the floor (see Appendix A-15).

La Raspa Variation
Students incorporate variations of the bleking step and create *foot* movements that make different sounds and *rhythms*.

Activity 7-5, continued

Rain Dance (3rd grade/older)

Native American dances ask for rain and good harvests as well as strength in battle. Incorporating variations of accented step hop movements in circle, line, and other spatial configurations, the dances are performed to drums and chanting (see Appendix A-16).

Rain Dance Variation

Students create a dance asking for something: rain, a good harvest, for spring to come. They use variations of accented and unaccented *rhythms* for step hop movements in different *geometric formations*.

Tanko Bushi (K/3rd grade) and **Tokyo Dontaku** (3rd grade/older)

These dances, from Japan, tell stories. The first illustrates the occupation of a coal miner and uses arm motions for digging and then throwing coal over one's shoulder with pauses to stop and rest. The second recounts going on a holiday. As part of the story-telling process the movements of these dances illustrate features of Japanese attire (see Appendix A-17).

Tanko Bushi and **Tokyo Dontaku Variations**

Students think of other occupations or another place to visit on holiday and create *body* movements to illustrate that occupation or trip.

Virginia Reel (3rd grade/older)

English colonists brought a version of this dance to the United States. Considered a weaving dance, dancers form two parallel lines and at one point travel as partners down the center of the lines. Popular during pioneer days to celebrate social events—including the raising of a neighbor's barn—the basic steps are also used in square dancing. Traditionally these dances were performed to fiddler music with steps announced by the caller, who might also be the fiddler (see Appendix A-18).

Virginia Reel Variation

Students learn traditional steps and formations, and then create their own variations of the *body* movements, and different *spatial configurations*. They take turns "calling" the dance and determining the dance's arrangement of steps or choreography.

Learning Outcomes:

Students demonstrate an understanding of a dance within its historical, cultural, and social context. Students reflect on the function of the dance as an expression of the people who created it. Students describe and compare the dances using the elements of dance. Students create their own variations based on the features of each dance and appreciate the variety of interpretations produced by their classmates.

As part of developing appreciation of these dances and their place in the lives of the people who created them, students can create their own folk dances.[6]

Activity 7-6
CHOREOGRAPH A FOLK DANCE

Age:
3rd grade/older
Time:
15–20 minutes

Music:
Several selections (see Appendix A-19, page 173)
Objectives:
To understand the function and structure of dances created by people in other places. To create an original folk dance with a beginning, middle, and end.

1. Place students in groups.
2. Create a mythical country. Discuss the climate, the people, their occupations, and other related features.
   Then
3. Decide the purpose of the dance. (example: "Land of Insomnia." Asking for sleep.)
4. Describe the emotions and feelings depicted in the dance.
   Then
5. Choose three descriptive words to identify the desired quality of movement (energy). (example: Wired, tired, restless.)
   Then
6. Create at least three different movements that relate to the theme. (example: Try to lie down, can't be still, can barely move.)
   Then
7. Choreograph a folk dance.
8. Decide the use of elements of space, time, energy, and body. (example: Personal space, all levels, curved pathways; slow, fast, syncopated; strong, light, sudden, sustained, direct, indirect, bound, free; non-locomotor gestures.)
9. The dance is 64 counts or one minute long. Select music or rhythm instruments to accompany the dance.
10. Begin and end the dance in the same configuration to restore order. (example: Sitting.)
    Then
11. Each group performs their dance and the class discusses all the various interpretations.

Learning Outcomes:
Students demonstrate the ability to create a dance by organizing dance ideas. They use descriptive words and variations of the elements of dance and their attributes to create the dance. They expand movement and verbal vocabularies as they develop creative thinking skills.

Dance Activities Can Integrate Other Arts

Besides studying dance as its own subject, dance as arts education also integrates other arts in dance activities. This occurs in two different ways: other arts can enhance or extend a dance performance, and/or they can inspire the original dance creation itself.

Each of the dance activities listed earlier in this chapter could incorporate extended arts activities as part of their study. For example each dance involved rhythmic accompaniment, either specific music or created rhythms. Also dances usually have a particular costume, piece of attire, or hand prop that is associated with them. Students can research these features and produce their own music and visual arts projects to enhance the dances. Students may also prepare creative writing projects to document their dance performance.

Arts Projects That Students Can Create to Enhance Their Dances

Drums and percussion instruments. Native American, African, and the New Zealand *Haka* dances all incorporate beats provided by stamping feet or various percussion instruments as accompaniment. Drums, ankle bells, rattles, and other percussion instruments can be made (see Appendix A–20).

Costume construction. Hawaiian dances utilize grass skirts, leis and flowers. The *Chicken Dance* can add beaks. The *Haka* dance often uses masks.

Hand prop construction. *Tanko Bushi* can use a shovel and many other dances have dancers manipulating fans and other hand-held props.

Performance documentation. Besides constructing items, there are additional drawing and writing activities to integrate other arts in dance study:

- Students draw pictures of themselves wearing appropriate attire and performing specific dances.

- Students write essays describing a dance performance in its original setting.

- Students compose poems describing their feelings about performing the dance.

- Students prepare time lines placing the dance in historical and cultural context.

- Students construct a dance manual describing the dance steps for students.

Various arts expressions can provide inspiration for creating dances. These
might include poetry, story telling, sculpture, paintings and other visual art forms, as
well as music and other sounds.

**Integration of
Other Arts as
Inspirations for
Dance Creation**

 Activity 7-7
POETRY

Age:
All ages
Time:
2-10 minutes

Materials:
Several poems (see Appendix A–21, page 173)
Objectives:
To explore the essence of a poem's expression using
movement. To create dances inspired by poetry.

1. Place students in groups.
2. Select poems by different poets that inspire movement.
3. Each group is given a different poem.
4. Students in groups design a moving picture to depict the essence,
   or the feeling of their poem.
   Then
5. Perform it for the class.
   Or
1. Select one poem.
2. Several groups interpret the same poem.
   Then
3. Perform their moving pictures to illustrate variety in interpretations.
   Or
1. Explore the rhythm provided by the words in the poem.
   Then
2. Create movements by parts of the body to follow the rhythm.
   Or
1. Encourage students to write poetry, possibly Haiku.
   Then
2. Create a dance to accompany it.
3. Add sound as desired.

Learning Outcomes:
Students integrate dance and poetry as arts education. They improvise with both
to create the other. They relate rhythm and poetry.

Activity 7-8
STORY TELLING

Age:
All ages
Time:
10–15 minutes

Materials:
Selected story (see Appendix A–22, page 173)
Objectives:
To tell a story with dance. To create a dance story using action words.

1. Students select a story they have been reading.
   Then
2. Individually or as a group, students choreograph a dance expressing the story.
   Or
1. Individual students select four action words.
   Then
2. Create a dance connecting the words with movement.
   Then
3. Share an action word dance with a partner.
   Then
4. Partners create an eight-count action word dance together.
   Then
5. Write a story using all eight action words in any order.

Learning Outcomes:
Students integrate dance and literature as arts education. They explore different ways to tell a story.

Activity 7-9
SCULPTURE

Age:
3rd grade/older
Time:
5-10 minutes

Objectives:
To introduce sculpture as an art form.
To create a dance based on a piece of sculpture.

1. Describe a piece of sculpture. (examples: Is it three dimensional; can it be created with any material?)
Then
2. In groups students assign themselves consecutive numbers.
Then
3. #1 is the first sculptor in each group. Other group members are the material.
4. The sculptor molds the material into an interpretation of suggested titles. (examples: Order, chaos, lonely, prickly, soaring, time out, friendship.)
5. Remind sculptors that their work is three-dimensional and can be seen from all sides.
Then
6. Groups freeze in their final form, and use peripheral vision to view the different expressions with the same title. Repeat until everyone has a turn to be the sculptor.
Or
1. Students individually form a piece of sculpture out of clay or other materials.
Then
2. Choreograph a dance of that sculpture.

Learning Outcomes:
Students create expressive three-dimensional forms with their bodies. They reinforce their understanding of shape as a means of expression.

Activity 7-10
PAINTING

Age:
3rd grade/older
Time:
15–20 minutes

Materials:
Several reproductions of artwork (see Appendix A-23 page 173)
Objectives:
To describe a painting using descriptive words and the elements of dance. To choreograph dances inspired by paintings.

1. Students in groups study reproductions of paintings from different times and places.
Then
2. Each group selects a painting to work with.
Then
3. Describe the painting using adjectives. (examples: Busy, calm, jagged.)
Then
4. Describe the painting using the elements of dance.
(example: What shapes, directions, levels, pathways are there? What body parts are accentuated? Describe the energy in the picture. Is there a rhythm? Syncopation? What is the tempo?)
Then
5. Using their answers to these questions, create a thirty-two count dance of the painting. (example: If the painting comes to life, how might it move?)
6. Dance should begin and end in a group configuration resembling the painting.
7. Select music or sound effects to complement the dance, and perform it.
Or
1. Students individually paint a picture.
Then
2. Place all the pictures in view.
Then
3. Each student selects one picture and choreographs a dance based on that picture.
Then
4. Classmates guess which picture was selected.

Learning Outcomes:
Students compare paintings and dance as forms of expression and consider each as an inspiration for the other.

Activity 7-11
MUSIC

Age:
All ages
Time:
2-5 minutes

Music:
Several selections (see Appendix A-24, page 174)
Objectives:
To move to a variety of rhythms and tempos.
To move like the structure of the music.
To discover music without lyrics.

1. Students move freely in general space to different music selections, varying in tempo, rhythm, and energy.
2. Move like the music makes them feel.

Or

1. Students can move like the structure of the music, or the sound of a particular instrument. (example: Moving high level on higher octave notes and low level on lower notes. Move to the time of individual notes, big slow steps for whole notes, faster steps for quarter notes, running steps for eighth notes.)

Or

1. Students freeze when the music stops.

Then

2. Dance when the music plays.

Then

3. Freeze while the music plays, and in the silence move like the music just heard.

Or

1. Students can bring in music for the class to use. (example: Challenge students to find music without lyrics, music with a variety of sound and accents, or music using unfamiliar instruments.)
2. Students choreograph dances or warm-up exercises to the music to be used in class.

Learning Outcomes:
Students concentrate on listening to music. They use music both to accompany and to create dances. They recognize the integration of music and dance.

Activity 7-12
SOUND EFFECTS

Age:
3rd grade/older
Time:
5-10 minutes

Sound Effects:
Several selections (see Appendix A-25, page 174)
Objectives:
To use environmental and created sounds as a source for
dance composition.

1. Select sounds from different environments: (example: Waves slapping on the shore, rain tapping on the window, machines operating full speed and winding down, fire engines with sirens sounding full blast, chirping crickets.)
Then
2. Students individually or in groups create movements to go with the sound, not necessarily depicting the source of the sound. (example: Move like the chirping cricket sound, but do not try to look like a cricket.)
Or
1. Students create their own sounds with body parts.
(example: Slapping thighs, snapping fingers, stomping feet.)
Then
2. Students choreograph movements to go with those sounds.

Learning Outcomes:
Students discover rhythms and expressive qualities in everyday familiar sounds and use those to improvise dance movements.

Additional variations for each of the activities above always appear once students begin thinking creatively. After each activity, reflect on the dances just made. What attributes of the elements of dance were used? How did the dance feel? How did classmates' interpretations differ? Encourage students to keep considering different ways to integrate arts expressions.

The Moving, Thinking, Willing, Feeling Child In previous chapters we defined dancing at school as providing physical education, kinesthetic reinforcement of learning, and cultural play. The first involves the moving child, the second engages the thinking child, and the third the willing child. Now we want to acknowledge the feeling child. Dancing at school is an activity that will potentially involve aspects of the whole child. In the first three, dancing activity is a method to achieve other goals. In the last instance dance is studied for its own value as an art–making process. All these objectives can be met at the same time depending on the particular methodology used by the teacher, as long as students are totally engaged.

> *I like to dance because it's like fire in my heart.*
> *When the music starts I go with the flow and all of a sudden*
> *I am dancing.*
>> *Student, eleven years old*

Notes for Chapter 7

1. This listing is a synthesis of objectives noted for dance as arts education in several documents including: *Visual and Performing Arts Framework for California Public Schools* (1996), "The Child's Bill of Rights in Dance" from *Standards for Dance in Early Childhood* (2003), and "What Children Should Know and Be Able to Do in the Arts" from the *National Standards for Dance Education* (1997).

2. Showing videos of the *Pavane* and of classical ballet examples, *after* students have created their dances, provides students with examples to compare with their own movement discoveries. When students are trying to understand the cultural context and aesthetics of an earlier dance form—rather than to authentically replicate the dance—showing videos after (rather than before) their creation is more challenging to their creative and critical thinking skills and avoids the attempt to replicate what they saw.

3. Again, showing videos of step, clog, or tap dancing *after* students have created their own rhythm stories, provides opportunities not only to compare the dance variations with their own, but also to try to comprehend the context within which these dances were created and the functions they served within that context.

4. Sensitivity toward dances from other cultures has two facets. The first involves the people who practice the dance as part of their culture and what meaning the dance has for them. Finding a resource, someone who knows the cultural aspects of the dance, to help with teaching the dance is a good way to answer any questions about specific religious or cultural traditions. The second facet involves students in the class who may have personal beliefs that may be in conflict with a particular dance. Teachers have told me that when they think a student may not wish to participate in a particular dance (because of ideological concerns), they send notices home, a week before, announcing what the class will be doing. Parents may prefer that their child have a study pass for that class. Each teacher has to make a decision about which dances to teach based on the cultural beliefs of students, and his or her own knowledge of the dance and what it means to the people who practice it.

5. When students are trying to learn a specific dance, showing a video of a performance before learning the dance may be helpful. Learning a specific dance has different objectives from the *Pavane* or Rhythm Stories activities cited above.

6. There are additional models for creating folk dances. See Lloyd, *Adventures in Creative Movement Activities,* pp. 205-212. Lloyd includes a model created and developed by dance educator Theresa Purcell Cone.

E I G H T

Observation

Consciously observing students' movement has taught me to be more diligent in my observations and therefore allows me to be more detailed in my written evaluations. In doing so, my evaluations can give more weight when expressing opinions about certain situations to my school parents.

Second grade teacher

Students' Non-verbal Movement Expression

Like their students, teachers assume several roles as active participants in the class-room: observer, creator, performer and reflector. While movement observation is an area of specialization within the broad field of dance education,[1] such information is helpful for educators as they observe their students' behavior—comparing and contrasting strengths, weaknesses, failures and successes—inside and outside the classroom.[2] Students' movement behavior, as non-verbal expression, generates material to use when creating dance lessons and when formulating classroom inter-action strategies.

Observation of a student's non-verbal movements (or lack of movement expression) provides insights about a student's mood or emotional feelings, physical health, personality features, motor development strengths and weaknesses, preferred learning styles, work effort, and social skills.[3]

Inappropriate behavior or an individual student's unusual movement behavior, whether or not it disturbs the class, may suggest that a student needs immediate assistance.

For example, I remember a young student who usually personified what every teacher desires: excellent behavior and enthusiastic participation in all activities.

One day she not only refused to join in the dancing, but became quite belligerent when anyone approached her. Two days later she was taken to the hospital with an unusual viral attack. Another young student was observed, on numerous occasions, standing still and gazing out the window rather than dancing. After describing this behavior to her parents, a medical examination discovered that the child was experiencing small seizures on a regular basis. Although both of these examples were corrected quickly with medical assistance, other expressions of undesired movement behavior need different types of intervention.

Recurring patterns of disruptive and inappropriate movement behavior may reflect developmentally weak performance of movement skills. These may include the following:

- Inability to distinguish left from right.
- Unable to stand or move in line without bumping into people in front or in back of them.
- Incapable of keeping one's hands under control.
- Failure trying to gallop, skip, jump on two feet, hop on one foot, or balance on one leg.
- Difficulty moving in the same direction as other students.
- Inability to slide across the room to one side and return on the other side without rotating.
- Inability to clap the rhythm of the music.
- Appearing to have no sense of the body moving as a whole.

Identifying these weaknesses through movement observation is important, for each of the aforementioned limitations can often be strengthened through fundamental motor skill exercises presented in dance sessions.

Observing students' movement behavior within group settings or alone can influence classroom management decisions. These may include the following:

- Where to seat students in relationship to one another.
- Who is left-handed and right-handed and may need more space on one side than the other?

- Who has difficulty mingling with others and often gets left out?
- Who is capable of leading?
- Who aggressively takes over leadership?

The teacher's observed movement of individual students provides details for evaluation descriptions for parents and supervisors.

Often specific details of movement behavior will trigger a memory for parents which they had noticed (such as the young girl experiencing seizures mentioned earlier) but had not considered particularly relevant. Or such a report may help parents watch for certain symptomatic behaviors (like a child who is unable to stand in line without bumping into the person in front or back of him, previously mentioned).

Teachers' Nonverbal Movement Expression and Self-Knowledge

Teachers can acquire aspects of self-knowledge as a result of thoughtfully observing their students' movement behavior. By observing how students approach them, teachers may assess the effect of their own nonverbal movement expression on students.

This includes how freely or openly students speak with them and choose to interact. What movement behavior, or body language, is the teacher exhibiting? Are arms and hands folded across the chest, placed on the hips, extended in a friendly gesture, or quietly held alongside the body? Is the approaching movement sudden and quick, or slower and relaxed? The amount of tension in a teacher's movement (bound or free flowing) has great impact on how students respond. Consider your movement behavior and non-verbal expression when interacting with students.

Teachers can ask themselves the following questions when conducting a class:

- How comfortable am I when physically moving?
- When standing in front of the class, do I prefer moving in personal space or traveling in general space?
- How far does my personal space extend around me?
- What parts of my body do I seem to use most?
- On what levels do I feel comfortable moving (do I bend down to talk to seated students)?

- What is my preferred tempo (am I always in a rush or am I "laid back")?

- Do I feel my muscles tense and tighten when I approach others, or do I feel relaxed?

- Would I describe my actions as focused or appearing distracted?

Answering these questions stimulates guidelines in preparing dance activities and lessons that include all attributes of the elements of dance, not just personal preferences of both teachers and their students. In these ways practicing movement observation expands everyone's movement vocabulary.

When and How to Use Movement Observation

Use the elements of dance (body, space, time, energy) and their attributes to describe observed movement behavior and expression. Identify a student to observe: for example, one who appears to have difficulty interacting with other students. Observe that student in different settings such as taking a test, playing outside at recess, eating lunch, or participating in group reading. Describe the student's movement behavior by answering the questions about teacher self-knowledge, listed above, applying them to the student. Consider the inappropriate movement behavior listed on page 112. Use those observations to determine appropriate behavior modifications.

Activity 8-1

HOW SLOWLY CAN YOU MOVE?

Age:
All ages
Time:
2 to 3 minutes

Objectives:
To calm hyperactive students who have difficulty sitting still, keeping their hands and arms under control, and settling down after active events.

1. Place students on one side of the room.
   Then
2. Challenge students to move slowly across the room. (example: Slow motion replay of a sports event.)
3. Participants must visibly keep moving their arms, legs, and whole body forward. (This does not mean just taking tiny steps.)
4. Student, moving continuously and slowly and taking the longest time to cross, wins.

Learning Outcomes:
Students concentrate on moving slowly and coordinating their movements and have fun doing it.

Activity 8-2
SIT USING NO HANDS

Age:
All ages
Time:
1 to 2 minutes

Objective:
To help students coordinate parts of their body.

1. Students stand in personal space.
   Then
2. Challenge students to find a way to slowly sit down on the floor without using their hands.
   Then
3. Stand up slowly without using their hands.

Learning Outcomes:
Students concentrate and enjoy the challenge of coordinating their body movement.

115

Activity 8-3
PUNCHING DANCE

Age:
All ages
Time:
2 to 3 minutes

Materials:
A balloon
Music:
Strong syncopated selection, no lyrics
Objective:
To help students with weak and indecisive movements be more assertive in their actions.

1. Place students in a circle.
   Then
2. Hold a balloon in front of them.
   Then
3. Students punch the balloon using different body parts.
   Then
4. Remove the balloon and students punch "air" with different body parts.
   Then
5. Keep changing body parts remaining in personal space.

Learning Outcome:
Students like and benefit from the opportunity to be more assertive and try to do so.

Activity 8-4
FLOATING DANCE

Age:
All ages
Time:
2 to 3 minutes

Music:
Light, flowing, smooth selection, no lyrics
Objectives:
To help students with rough and aggressive movements channel their energy into producing lighter, more sensitive actions.

1. Place students around the room.
   Then
2. Imagine blowing soap bubbles. Try to keep them from falling to the floor.
   Then
3. Students imagine soap bubbles in front of them.
4. Use different body parts to keep them from touching the floor or bursting.

Learning Outcome:
Students benefit from the opportunity to concentrate on lighter, less aggressive responses.

Activity 8-5
SKIP REVIEW (see page 33)

Age:
All ages
Time:
1 to 2 minutes

Objective:
To assist older students who continue to have difficulty skipping and shifting their weight.

1. Students stand in personal space.
   Then
2. Exaggerate marching in place. Lift high one knee and then the other. Say "step, lift;" "step, lift."
3. Be sure students completely shift weight from one leg to the other on each step.
   Then
4. Move among students. Stand next to or in front of students having difficulty.
   Then
5. Add a hop on the supporting leg during each lift. Repeat "step, lift, hop" on each leg.
   Then
6. Increase tempo. Begin skipping around the room.

Learning Outcome:
Students appreciate the opportunity to work on a skill that is often difficult and therefore embarrassing to them.

Activity 8-6
JUMP REVIEW (see page 32)

Age:
All ages
Time:
2 to 3 minutes

Objective:
To help students who have difficulty establishing a rhythm for jumping (which may include unsuccessful attempts at jumping rope).

1. Students stand in personal space.
   Then
2. Begin clapping even beats (or striking a drum).
   Then
3. Pretend to bounce a ball with both hands.
   Then
4. Add bouncing bodies, slightly bending and straightening both knees.
   Then
5. When bouncing is rhythmically even, eliminate bouncing hands. Leave the floor with small jumps after each bounce of the knees.
   Then
6. Gradually continue jumping and adding height.

Learning Outcome:
Students benefit from the emphasis on rhythm when trying to improve jumping skills.

Activity 8-7
TAKE THEIR LEAD

Age:
All ages
Time:
1 to 2 minutes

Objective:
To assist students who consistently sit quietly and alone off to the side.

1. Approach the student on the same spatial level by sitting down next to him or her, for example. (However, not too close until you sense the student's spatial comfort zone.)
2. Gradually gain his or her confidence.
   Then
3. Team them with another, also quiet, student.
4. Gradually involve both with other less quiet but accommodating students.

Learning Outcome:
Students like to be included.

Activity 8-8
RIGHT AND LEFT REVIEW

Age:
All ages
Time:
1 to 2 minutes

Objective:
To assist students who slide sideways in one direction across the floor and when asked to return in the other direction, turn their body 180 degrees to return (thus repeating the same side of the body leading).

1. Place students in a line formation.
   Then
2. With your back to students, slide across the floor to the right side.
   Then
3. Still with your back to students, without turning return to the other side of the room, this time sliding to the left side.
   Then
4. Repeat with students and say the side ("right" or "left") that is leading each time.

Learning Outcome:
Students strengthen their locomotor and physical development using both sides of the body.

Each of the foregoing activities includes the elements of dance. For example, Activities 8-1, 8-2, 8-5, and 8-6 target timing of the movement and coordinating the body accordingly; Activities 8-3 and 8-4 focus on the use of energy and coordinating the body; and Activities 8-7 and 8-8 target sharing general space.

Applying the elements of dance to everyday movement of a child in different settings was insightful. Considering such elements helps to understand how to interact with students and speak to them. I was amazed to see just how much a child moves in a short period of time, and how much the elements of dance movement are present in all aspects of life.

Third grade teacher

Notes for Chapter 8

1. Certification courses in movement observation are offered through Laban/Bartenieff Institute of Movement Studies, Inc. in New York City, as well as programs offered through dance departments of several universities in the United States. Movement analysis, as a field of study, was inspired by the work of dance educator and theorist, Rudolf Laban, who is also known for introducing his theories of modern educational dance to the British Primary Schools in the 1950s (see Chapter 3, p. 13). Additional contributions of Laban to the field of dance include his system of movement notation, called Labanotation, which is used for the preservation and reconstruction of dance choreographies (see Chapter 3, Note 2).

2. Currently some classroom teachers, attempting to support change in teaching environments or instructional methodology, are conducting in-classroom action research. Reviews of some of these studies are found in the Research in Dance Education database (www.ndeo.org/research). Begin with "educational issue" categories: kinesthetic learning, learning theory, arts education; "population served" categories: early childhood, K–4; and "area of service" category: pedagogy. Additionally the National Dance Education Organization as part of the scope of its mission initiates training programs for dance and other arts educators who wish to pursue support for their programs via research. For more information regarding current NDEO research projects go to www.NDEO.org.

3. For example, Marion North, a student and associate of Rudolf Laban in London, utilized movement observation as a research tool to study the personalities of several children during creative dance classes she taught one school year. For the results of her study, which correlated her findings to the children's academic achievements, see North, *Personality Assessment through Movement*.

NINE

Creating Dance Lesson Plans for the Classroom

I like the challenge of creating dance lessons for my class. I especially like the fact that I can choose subjects that tie in with what I am teaching.

   Second grade teacher

A goal of dance experience in school is that students will develop creative thinking skills.

Teachers providing dance lessons have already chosen to be innovative and creative in their thinking and their teaching. This choice involves preparing lesson plans that will guide the students toward thinking creatively and making divergent choices for themselves as they expand their movement vocabulary and dance experience. With most students this will necessitate more guidance than simply playing some music and instructing the class to move the way the music makes them feel.

Structure for Dance Lesson Plans

This chapter discusses dance lesson plan format and possible content. A distinction is now made between dance lesson plans, which this chapter describes, and the single dance activities presented in previous chapters. Presented were single activities (rather than lesson plans) as first steps toward expanding individual movement vocabularies and developing familiarity with dance terminology. However, Activities 6-11 (Hip Hop), 7-3 (17th Century Walking Dance), and 7-4 (Rhythm Stories) in Chapters 6 and 7 were exceptions, in that all three were presented as a longer lesson, leading up to the material in this chapter. Strategies to engage students, control measures, and assessment procedures—all of which are important to successfully implement dance lessons at school—are not detailed in this chapter, but will be discussed in Chapters 10 and 11.

A dance lesson can be divided into four parts: warm-up/introduction, skill reinforcement/review, culminating activity/student application, and cool-down/closure/reflection.

The warm-up and cool-down portions of dance lessons at school may be very different from dance classes and exercise sessions in dance studios because dance in school settings will not usually involve as much physical exertion.[1] However, school dance sessions still need an introduction or warming up to the activity as well as a cooling down or closing.

The warm-up/introduction portion of the lesson may or may not include a broad range of activities.

- Generally participants perform or remain in personal space.
- Teachers may introduce the lesson focus or objective through discussion.
- Participants may or may not demonstrate proposed movement examples.
- Participants may or may not move the body or body parts to prepare for moving.
- The extent of the physical energy expended during this portion of the lesson depends on the design and objectives of the specific lesson.

The skill reinforcement/review portion of the lesson usually involves full body movement.

- Participants usually move in general space and expend more physical energy.
- Students explore and reinforce movement themes/concepts presented in the warm-up/introduction of the lesson.
- Students may also review movements or sequences previously learned.
- Teachers guide the activity and structure its process during this portion of the lesson.

Students make their own movement choices and apply their learning during the culminating activity.

- Students use general space to create within the instructed parameters.

- Students may work as one large group, in small groups, individually, or with partners.

- Students creatively apply the lesson, and solve whatever problems the teacher provides.

- Students present their solutions to the class as a whole so that all students recognize a variety of solutions to the same problem.

Cool-down/closure completes the lesson, provides reflection on the lesson, and may include a range of activities.

- Participants remain in personal space.

- Students may perform slow stretching as needed.

- Students reflect on, discuss, and assess what they have learned and performed.

- They will discuss each presentation in terms of the use of the elements of dance.

- They will describe and compare individual feelings and interpretations as creators, performers, and observers.

- There is no high-exertion physical activity during cool-down/closure.

- Participants close the lesson, and prepare to move on to another activity.

Generally, this format of warm-up/introduction, skill reinforcement/review, culminating activity/student application, and cool-down/closure/reflection can be used as the structure for creating dance lesson plans. The amount of time devoted to each section will depend on the age group and the particular lesson at hand.

There are four important principles to remember when planning dance lessons:

- Identify clear objectives and learning outcomes using national or state standards as guidelines.

- Establish a common ground, something familiar to engage students' initial interest.

- Provide opportunity for all students to participate, to express themselves, and to use creative and critical thinking skills.

125

• Include several attributes of the four dance elements.

**Dance Lesson
Plan Samples**

Several lesson plan outlines follow, employing this format and illustrating the four important principles. First is a specific lesson plan for younger students, and then several for varying ages. Each one is designed as a model to suggest multiple possibilities to be developed through teachers' individual creativity.

While reading this lesson plan for younger students, try to use it as a springboard to imagine similar activities of greater or lesser complexity for other age groups, including special populations.

Activity 9-1
FULL LESSON PLAN
A TRIP TO THE PLAYGROUND

Age:
Pre-K/K
Time:
15 to 20 minutes

Materials:
Masking tape (see Appendix A-26, page 174)
Music:
Playful music in background
Objectives:
To create a dance story about a shared experience.
To involve all students in the creative process.

Introductory Preparation:
Place masking tape X marks (one for each student) on the floor
in a circle.

Warm-up/Introduction and Skill Reinforcement/Review

1. Students find personal space—the area that can be reached in all directions from the center of the body—and sit on the floor in a circle.
2. Ask students to raise their hands to establish how many have ever been to a playground.
3. Go around the circle asking each student to share their favorite playground activity. (example: Swings, sandbox, teeter-totter, slide.)
4. Ask students specific questions about their choice. (example: "What parts of your body do you use when you _____? How do you move those body parts? Do you _____ fast or slow? Do you _____ up in the air or down on the ground?)
5. As needed, have students demonstrate the movement they are describing.

Activity 9-1, continued
Culminating Activity/Students Apply the Lesson
1. The group spreads out in general space.
2. They lie down on the floor as if they are sleeping and about to wake up in the morning.
3. The teacher moves with the students, narrating and demonstrating the following: (example: Wake up and stretch different body parts. Stand up, stretch again, make the bed, fluff the pillows. Wash face, brush teeth, comb hair, and get dressed to go to the playground.)
4. Sit around the breakfast table. (example: Drink juice, eat favorite breakfast food. Remind students to chew and swallow and use a napkin.)
5. Stand up and push chair under the table.
6. Everyone walks or skips or dances to the playground moving around the room. (example: Look up at the sun, the trees, and down at the flowers along the way.)
7. Arriving at the playground, jump into the sandbox. (example: Cover legs with sand; wiggle toes, knees, legs and shake off the sand. Build a sand castle or sand person. Brush off the sand and stand up shaking it off.)
8. Proceed to next activity in a different part of the room.
9. Place hands on the chains of the swing. (example: Move forward and backward getting higher each time. Jump off the swing. Push a friend in the swing, being careful to get out of the way of the swing.)
10. Move to the jungle gym (or parallel bars) in another area. (example: Climb up on the jungle gym or parallel bars. Travel across using arms and hands. Climb down at the other side or end.)
11. Move to the slide. (example: Scoot across the room on bottom or stomach.)
12. Find an (imaginary) ball. (example: Bounce it, throw it, catch it, roll it, kick it using both legs, dodge it.)
13. Play jump rope or hop scotch.
14. With partners sit on the teeter totter (seesaw). (example: One rises as the other lowers.)
15. Everyone repeats their favorite activity, mentioned during the warm-up.
16. Finally, climb on the merry-go-round. (example: Gallop in a circle increasing tempo, then slow down, and stop.)
17. Walk home slowly. It has been a long tiring day at the playground.
18. At home, lie down to take a nap before lunch. (example: Dream about trip to the playground.)

Cool-down/Closure/Reflection
1. Tap each student on the toe when it is time to return to his or her seat in the circle.
2. Discuss the trip to the playground. (example: What activities did they like the best? What parts of the body did they use? Did they like moving fast or slow? What directions did they travel in? Which activities took the most energy and tired them out?)
3. Students quietly move on to another activity.

Activity 9-1, continued
Learning Outcomes:
Students relate dance movement to their everyday lives. They reinforce story format. They strengthen body part identification, locomotor skills, spatial and temporal orientation, and work in both personal and general space. They expand movement and verbal vocabulary. Each student contributes to the creative process.

A trip to the playground is a good theme for the first creative dance session with young children, and it satisfies the four principles listed on pages 125-126.

Identifying clear objectives and learning outcomes. It follows the standards for preschool and elementary school dance education (see Appendix B-1) as guidelines for structuring dance lessons to fulfill specific objectives and essential learning outcomes of what students should know and be able to do in dance education.

Establishing a common ground. Every young child has gotten up in the morning, performed a morning routine, and visited some sort of a playground and therefore can relate to the activity. After years of experiences in differing geographical and socioeconomic areas, I have learned that not every child has been to a zoo nor has every child, even in southern California, been to Disneyland. However, all young children seem to have visited a playground. By selecting a common ground such as a playground, teachers provide opportunities for all students to contribute ideas in developing the group's creative dance.

Involving all students in the process of developing the creative dance. Every child has the opportunity to suggest their favorite activity and provide details that are personally significant. Teachers can then validate those choices by including them in the activity. Providing children opportunities to make choices and then to see their choices materialize as part of the group's activity is an important first step toward nurturing creative thinking skills.

The playground activity incorporates the elements of dance. Different *body parts* and their movements are stressed both in initial discussion and during the activities. *Personal and general space* are interchanged and used through-out. *Levels* of the body are used: high when jumping, swinging, and on the teeter-totter; low when sliding on the slide, sitting at the table, playing in the sandbox, and sleeping; and middle as they move around the room. *Directions* are included: forward and backward on the swing, sideways catching the ball. *Pathways* include: curved on the merry-go-round, straight on the slide, zigzag when dodging the ball. Different body *shapes* are formed sitting in a circle and making sand people in the sandbox. The element of time includes *tempo* changes throughout: walking home slowly, accelerating/decelerating on the merry-go-round. *Duration* involves the length of the trip itself. *Rhythm* occurs during jumping and bouncing activities. *Energy* appears in different movement qualities: fluff the pillow, push the chair under the table, push your friend in the swing, pack the sand around your legs, throw the ball. Additionally, several *locomotor* skills are included: walking, galloping, skipping, jump-ing and hopping.

Once common ground has been established, children contribute ideas for the creative process. They will then be ready to try creative dance trips to other, not as familiar, places.

Using the playground trip as a model, other dance stories might include going to the beach, visiting the zoo, entering a rain forest, or even traveling to the moon. Dance stories for all ages can also revolve around recounting everyday events.

For example, Hawaiian dances describe attending a luau, going fishing, looking at the ocean, swaying palm trees, and distant volcanoes. Beginning and ending the dance trip, by enacting getting up each morning and returning home afterward, reinforces a sense of story for young children.

The following are lesson plans for varying age groups. They are listed with reference to the elements of dance they emphasize; using these elements—both as a means to develop dance lessons and also to describe dance activity—is an impor-tant feature of creating dance lessons as arts education. The following lessons also provide opportunities for all students to be involved in the creative process and they utilize initial common grounds. Also, they include specific objectives and learning outcomes. Consider each of the following as a springboard for possible variations with adaptations for other age groups.

**Dance Lesson
Plans for Varying
Age Groups**

Activity 9-2
FULL LESSON PLAN
BE A MARIONETTE
BODY PARTS

Age:
Pre–K/K
Time:
7 to 10 minutes

Materials:
A marionette
Objectives:
Reinforce body part identification. Involve students in
the creative process.

Warm-up/Introduction

1. Students sit in personal space.
2. Introduce the job of a puppeteer who moves marionettes.
   (example: Demonstrate, using a marionette.)
3. Describe a marionette with strings attached to its body parts. (example:
   Demonstrate, using a marionette.)
4. Identify body parts that might have strings attached. (example: All joints.)

Skill Reinforcement/Review

1. All students stand and practice being a marionette as teacher
   calls out various parts. (examples: Hang by your back, your ankle, your
   shoulder, fall in a heap.)

Culminating Activity/Students Apply the Lesson

1. Students take turns being the puppeteer (as all classmates are marionettes).
2. Puppeteer calls out different body parts to hang by.
3. Puppeteer designates different movements for each part.
4. Puppeteer designates tempo for each movement.

Cool-down/Closure/Reflection

1. Students identify different body parts used and movements of each.
2. Discuss which role they liked best (marionette or puppeteer) and why.

Learning Outcomes:

Students experience being a leader and a follower. Body part identification,
non-locomotor movement, and changes in tempo are reinforced.

Activity 9-3

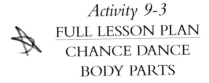

FULL LESSON PLAN
CHANCE DANCE
BODY PARTS

Age:
3rd grade/older
Time:
15 to 20 minutes

Materials:
Dice
Music:
Drum (see Appendix A-20, page 173)
Objectives:
To create dance sequences of different durations.
To expand movement and verbal vocabularies.

Warm–up/Introduction
1. Describe and discuss movement possibilities of different body parts.
2. The class, as a whole, selects six body parts. Assign numbers and movements to each. Write on chalkboard for reference. (example: 1. thrusting hip, 2. pointing finger, 3. bending knee, 4. rolling shoulder, 5. turning head, 6. stamping foot.)

Skill Reinforcement/Review
1. Place students in groups of five or six.
2. Groups explore variations for each of the six movements and their respective body parts.
3. Give each group a die, which they toss six times.
4. The tosses of the die determine the order of the six numbered movements. (example: First toss is "5," therefore first movement of routine is 5, turning head.)
5. Establish a steady even beat of six counts using a drum or clapping.
6. Each group prepares six counts of movement.
7. Order is determined by the numbers of the die tosses. (example: First toss is "5," second toss is "2," third toss is "1," etc. The movement is turning head, pointing finger, thrusting hip, etc.)
8. Groups perform their six counts for the class.

Culminating Activity/Students Apply the Lesson
1. Groups extend their six counts of movement to sixteen counts using same tempo. (example: Repeat single movements within the sequence; repeat the whole sequence two plus times; or change tempo within the sequence, slowing down some of the movements to take more than one count.)
2. Groups use the same order, body parts and movements as their six counts of movement.

Activity 9-3, continued

3. Groups perform for the class.
4. Students guess strategy used to extend the movement from six to sixteen counts. (example: Repeat single movements within the sequence, repeat the whole sequence two plus times, or change tempo within the sequence, slowing down some of the movements to take more than one count.)
5. Groups create another sixteen counts of movement.
6. The movements, the order, and the tempo of the steady beat are the same, but the moving body part changes. (example: They might change "turning head" to turning foot.)
7. Groups perform for the class.

Cool-down/Closure/Reflection

1. Students discuss their dances using elements of dance. (example: Different body parts used when they changed body parts. How those different parts affected the movement. How changing the tempo and duration of movements provided variations.)
2. They consider other possible variations for this movement problem.

Learning Outcomes:

Students work in groups. They experience contrasting movements for different body parts. They explore variations in the element of time. They create dance sequences of varying duration: six and sixteen counts. They see different interpretations of the same movement problems.

Lesson Plans/Activities 9–2 and 9–3 incorporate many attributes of dance elements. Both emphasize the *body* and its parts. *Time* is a secondary emphasis. In Be a Marionette it appears as *tempo* changes and in Chance Dance it extends the six counts of movement to sixteen counts, which involves both *duration* of the movements and *tempo* variations. *Personal space* rather than general space will most likely be used for both activities. Although different spatial configurations, involving pathways, directions, and shapes will occur, space as an element of dance will not be as emphasized in the students' minds as the body parts used. *Energy* expended may be reflected in added musical accompaniment.

Activity 9-4
FULL LESSON PLAN
CIRCLE DANCE
SHAPE AND SPACE
(ALSO STRAIGHT LINE OR OTHER SPECIFIC GEOMETRIC SHAPE DANCE)

Age:	**Music:**
K/3rd grade	A waltz rhythm
Time:	**Objectives:**
10 minutes	To reinforce circle shapes, curved pathways and movement.

3   4

Warm-up/Introduction

1. Introduce curved *shapes* and circles.
2. Students sitting in personal space look around the room and identify circles and circular objects they see.
3. Students form circles with different body parts.
   (examples: Draw a circle with your chin, form a circle with your arms.)
4. Students remain in personal space to form curved shapes using their whole body.

Skill Reinforcement/Review

1. Students follow the teacher walking on a curved pathway.
2. They form one large circle together.
3. Students walk in their own circles, gradually increase circles in size in general space.
4. Challenge students to move circularly.
5. Experiment with changing levels, tempos, and amounts of energy used while making curved shapes with their bodies. (example: Form a circle close to the floor, very quickly, strongly and suddenly.)

3

Activity 9-4, continued

Culminating Activity/Students Apply the Lesson

1. Divide students into partners. Number the partners #1 and #2.
   #1s will observe first while #2s create a Circle Dance to approximately
   one minute of music.
   #1s will count the number of circles they see in their partner's dance.
   #2s begin and end their dance in their own Circle Dance body shape
   or pose.
2. Select music with an even rhythm, perhaps a waltz rhythm.
3. As needed, challenge #2s to think of all the ways they can make circles:
   (example: Using different body parts, moving like a circle, moving in a circle.)
4. After the dance performance ask for a raise of hands for numbers
   of circles seen. (example: How many saw ten circles, fifteen, etc.)
5. Repeat the process with #1s dancing and #2s observing.

Cool-down/Closure/Reflection

1. Students sit in personal space on the floor in a circle. Discuss the dances.
2. Some may demonstrate circles their partner formed they especially liked.
3. Try to describe what a circle looks like.
4. Recall different ways to make circles, and different body parts to use.
5. Demonstrate curved pathways.
6. Discuss how circle dances made them feel.

Learning Outcomes: Students experience circular shapes and movements.
They improvise a dance with a beginning, middle, and end. They observe and
compare variations in forming circles. They reflect on their own feelings about
circular movement.

Straight line or other geometric shape dances provide variations for the
Circle Dance. Use music to contrast the movement of one shape with another. For
example, a waltz rhythm works well with a circle dance and a straight line dance
may use a march rhythm with staccato accents. Follow contrasting dances such as
Circle Dance and Straight Line Dance with discussion. Challenge students to compare the two, to discuss which they personally enjoyed the most and what may have
influenced their choice.

Activity 9-5
FULL LESSON PLAN
NAME DANCE
SHAPE AND SPACE

Age:
1st grade/older
Time:
10 to 12 minuteS

Music:
Drum (see Appendix A-20, page 173)
Objectives:
To form concrete shapes of the letters of the alphabet
with bodies. To contrast tempo and energy while moving
from one shape to another.

Warm-up/Introduction
1. Discuss shaping the body and its parts to form geometric shapes.
2. In personal space form circles and straight lines with different isolated
   body parts. (example: Hands, arms, legs.)
3. Form circles and straight lines with full body standing, sitting,
   and lying on the floor.

Skill Reinforcement/Review
1. Form specific letters of the alphabet with single body parts and then
   with the full body. (examples: X, T, A, M, Z. Gradually increase complexity.
   Change body levels: standing, sitting, lying on the floor.)
2. Students work with partners and form single letters using two bodies.
   (example: O, M, T. Change body levels.)

Culminating Activity/Students Apply the Lesson
1. Ask students to count the number of letters in their own name.
2. Strike a drum (or clap).
3. Each student spells his or her own name forming one letter for each beat.
4. Repeat, using different levels of the body to gain contrast in body shapes.
5. Repeat, accelerating the tempo.
6. Suggest variations in movement quality. (example: Move smoothly as if
   writing in cursive, abruptly as if using a computer.)
7. Repeat activity, spelling name backwards.

Cool-down/Closure/Reflection
1. Sitting in personal space, discuss forming the different letters. (example:
   Which body shapes were more difficult, which did they like to form, which
   were especially creative?)
2. How did they feel using body spelling?
3. Which do they prefer: body spelling or written spelling? Why?

Activity 9-5, continued

Learning Outcomes: Students find different ways to form the same concrete shape using different body parts and the whole body. Students work with partners to form letter shapes. Students use different levels, changing tempo, and contrasting energy expenditure. Students contribute their observations and feelings about the activity.

Activity 9-5 is a good introduction to creative dance lessons for all elementary age students above kindergarten. Spelling one's name with movement gives each student the opportunity to find different movement solutions, and thus feel successful. Additionally, concentrating on how to form the shapes of concrete letters rather than moving abstractly may be less intimidating to novice dancers. Challenging students to form concrete shapes (letters of the alphabet and geometric shapes) with their bodies is a first step toward asking students to create their own abstract shapes, such as those asked for in the following Lesson Plan/Activity 9-6.

Depending on the complexity of their names, Lesson Plan/Activity 9-5 works well with many first graders. However, not wanting to frustrate students who may have longer, more difficult names to body spell, first grade teachers may substitute words—other than individual names—for spelling in this lesson plan. Body spelling individual names is particularly good for older students who have not participated in creative dance activities or lessons before and are hesitant to try.

Activity 9-6
FULL LESSON PLAN
JIGSAW PUZZLE
SHAPE AND SPACE

Age:
3rd grade/older
Time:
15 to 20 minutes

Music:
Flowing continuous pattern, no lyrics
Objectives:
To form abstract shapes. To improvise body contours.
To share general space with others.

Warm-up/Introduction
1. Discuss and identify concrete and abstract shapes.
2. In personal space students form different abstract body shapes.
   (example: Symmetrical, asymmetrical, open, closed, jagged, or smooth.)
3. Define and describe jigsaw puzzles and their pieces. (example: Different sizes
   and shapes of pieces that fit together to form a picture.)

Skill Reinforcement/Review
1. Place students in partners.
2. With their bodies, each pair creates three different puzzle piece
   shapes that fit together.
3. Practice moving into and out of the shapes slowly and smoothly,
   and then quickly and jaggedly.

Culminating Activity/Students Apply the Lesson
1. Divide students into groups of six or seven people.
2. Number each person #1 through
   #6 or #7.
3. #1 forms a body shape of
   his/her choosing.
4. In numerical order, each student, **without touching the other students,**
   adds a body shaped piece to the developing puzzle by filling empty spaces.
5. After each person has had a turn to add
   to the first puzzle, immediately begin
   forming a second puzzle. (example:
   Students remain in their puzzle shapes
   until it is their turn to move again.)
6. This time #2 moves to a different place in the room and forms a new body
   shape. #3, #4, #5, #6, #7, and #1 follow.

4

137

Activity 9-6, continued

7. Repeat the sequence until each person has had a chance to begin a puzzle.

8. Encourage the class to move quickly and spontaneously to keep the puzzle flowing. Use music to motivate continual movement.

9. Divide the class in half. One half is the audience, while the other half in groups of 6 or 7 form puzzles. Then reverse roles.

Cool-down/Closure/Reflection

1. Students in personal space discuss what they experienced.
   (example: While forming the puzzles—which shapes felt good, which were uncomfortable? Describe shapes as symmetrical, etc.)

2. Students describe what they saw happening.
   (example: When observing—which shapes were interesting, which seemed original? Describe shapes as symmetrical, etc. What body levels were used?)

3. Discuss differences they noticed between the first and the last puzzles formed.
   (example: Often pieces become more interesting or creative as puzzles progress and participants become more comfortable.)

Learning Outcomes:

Students improvise and move quickly and spontaneously. They form contrasting abstract shapes. They work as a group to create a group shape.

Activities 9-4, 9-5, and 9-6 incorporate many attributes of the elements of dance. All three emphasize the elements of space and the body. Body shapes and levels are prominent. Noticeable changes in directions and pathways are also actively involved during the Circle Dance and Jigsaw Puzzle Dance. Concentration on the use of body parts is most evident during the Circle Dance and the Name Dance. Tempo and rhythm of the dances is emphasized by music or accompaniment used during all the lessons. The number of letters in each name and the time involved for each puzzle formation determines duration of those dances. Variations in energy expenditure are individually applied but can also be suggested by teachers' instructions such as "move quickly," "smoothly," or "suddenly." Description of these dance elements can be discussed during reflection.

Activity 9-7

FULL LESSON PLAN

FOLLOW THE BEAT OF THE DRUM

TIME AND TEMPO

Age:
Pre K/K
Time:
Time: 5 to 8 minutes

Music:
Drum (see Appendix A-20, page 173)
Objectives:
To reinforce listening. To strengthen locomotor skills:
walking and running. To share general space with others.

Warm–up/Introduction
1. Place students around the room.
2. Instruct them to listen to the drum beats.
3. Students move when they hear the drum, freeze when it is silent.
4. Practice several times, moving to the drum, freezing when it stops.

Skill Reinforcement/Review
1. Strike the drum slowly, demonstrating big steps to the slow beat.
   Students follow.
2. Strike the drum faster, demonstrating walking steps to the faster beat.
   Students follow.
3. Strike the drum even faster, demonstrating running steps to the even faster
   beat. Students follow.
4. Encourage students to say "big steps," "walking steps," and "running steps" as
   they perform them.
5. Play four slow beats and perform big steps.
6. Play eight faster beats and walk. Play sixteen even faster beats and run.
   (example: Think musically: four half notes, eight quarter notes, sixteen eighth
   notes.)
7. Repeat several times.

Culminating Activity/Students Apply the Lesson
1. Divide the class into three groups.
2. One group is big steppers, one is walkers, and one is runners.
3. Practice several times with students moving when they hear their tempo.
4. Then let each student choose the tempo he or she wants to move to.
5. Play the drum and each moves when he or she hears the chosen tempo.
6. Finally repeat four slow steps, eight walking steps, sixteen running steps, and
   add thirty-two very fast running steps.
7. Students close into a small circle.
8. Stop. Inhale deeply through the nose and exhale through the mouth.

Activity 9-7, continued

Cool-down/Closure/Reflection

1. Students sit in personal space and reflect.
2. Discuss the importance of listening.
   (example: When to move, when to stop, which step to do.)
3. Discuss moving in general space versus personal space.
4. Discuss differences between the steps.
   (example: Steps increased in tempo and decreased in size.)
5. Which step did they like best and why?
6. As applicable, connect music time values of half, quarter, and sixteenth notes with steps.

Learning Outcomes:

Students concentrate on listening and sharing space with others. Students recognize and move to different tempos. Students choose which step/tempo they prefer and reflect on why.

Variations for this activity would allow individual students to play the drum and to select which tempo to play. This variation could occur during the Lesson 9-7 above or at another time, depending on the attention span of the students.

Activity 9-8
FULL LESSON PLAN
CHANGING TEMPO AND RHYTHM
TIME AND RHYTHM

Age:
3rd grade/older
Time:
20 to 25 minutes

Music:
Drum (see Appendix A-20, page 173, upbeat music, no lyrics)
Objectives:
To think creatively. To vary tempos and create rhythms. To work with groups.

Warm-up/Introduction

1. Introduce/review the dance element, *time*, and its five attributes (Chapter 3, pages 16-17).
2. Standing, feet together, arms down, in personal space, students count out loud.
3. Count four counts, as arms stretch to the ceiling, alternate first one arm and then the other.
4. Arms are down alongside body.
5. Count four counts as top of head rolls down toward the floor, upper body curving forward, ending up hanging at the waist.

Activity 9-8, continued

6. Count four counts as torso straightens, and stretch torso and arms forward from the hips, parallel to the floor.
7. Count four counts as knees bend and the body curves (elbows next to knees), straighten knees and roll body up to standing position.
   Then
8. Step one leg to the side. Counting sixteen counts, repeat #3 through #7.
   Then
9. Place feet and legs together momentarily, then move one leg forward several inches.
10. Counting sixteen counts, repeat exercise.
    Then
11. Place feet and legs together momentarily, then move other leg forward several inches.
12. Counting sixteen counts, repeat #3 through #7.
    Then
13. Repeat #3 through #7 in all four leg positions.(example: Legs together, one foot steps side, one foot steps forward, other foot forward.)
14. Count two counts for each movement (instead of four) for a total of eight counts per position.
15. Tempo of counts remains the same, students count out loud.
    Then
16. Repeat #3 through #7 again in all four leg positions.
17. Count one count for each movement (instead of two) for a total of four counts per position.
18. Tempo of counts remains the same, students count out loud.
19. Inform students they just changed the tempo of their movements in this exercise.

Skill Reinforcement/Review
1. Place students in columns to move across the floor one column at a time.
2. One student plays a steady pulse on the drum. Change students playing the drum often.
3. First row walks forward four steps, (1, 2, 3, 4). Then freeze four counts (5, 6, 7, 8).
4. Each row begins eight counts after the previous row.
   Then
5. First row walks forward four steps, (1, 2, 3, 4). Gesture using one body part one count (5), freeze three counts (6, 7, 8).
6. Each row begins eight counts after the previous row.
   Then
7. First row walks forward four steps, (1, 2, 3, 4). Gesture using one body part one count (5), moving the whole body on two counts (6, 7) and freezes one count (8).
8. Each row begins eight counts after the previous one.
9. Inform students they created their own rhythm, while the drummer provided the pulse for the eight count sequences.

141

Activity 9-8, continued

Culminating Activity/Students Apply the Lesson

1. Divide class in groups of five students each.
2. Assign numbers 1 to 5.
3. Each number receives two relationship words for which they create whole body repetitive actions. Envision that they are parts of an imaginary machine as they create its rhythm. (example: #1 up and down, #2 around and through, #3 in and out, #4 near and far, #5 over and under.)
4. Call out the numbers for each student to begin their repetitive movement. (example: #5, #1, #3, … in any order.)
5. Once everyone is moving and relating to each other's movements, vary the cues. (example: Make one movement light and the other strong. Make one movement sudden and the other sustained.)
6. Continue to vary cues. (example: #1 and #5 begin to move erratically, #2 and #3 gradually accelerate. #4 gradually decelerates until hardly moving at all. #1 accelerates to moving rapidly. #5 completely stops for three counts and then starts suddenly. Keep repeating pattern. #2 and #4 move erratically. #5 gradually decelerates.)
7. Everyone stops.

Cool-down/Closure/Reflection

1. In personal space students discuss their dances.
2. Identify presence of the five attributes of the element of *time* in their lesson. (example: Tempo, rhythm, pulse, syncopation, and duration.)
3. Reflect on the changes in tempo and rhythm they performed. (example: Stretching exercises increased tempo, walking exercise created their own rhythm, machines created rhythm, and changed the tempo.)
4. Discuss the machines they created: similarities and contrasts in created rhythms, use of tempo and syncopation, and how energy changes are also related to tempo and rhythm.

Learning Outcomes:

Students reinforce the dance element of time and all of its attributes. They change tempos and create their own rhythms while moving. Additionally they experience variations in energy expenditure.

Activities 9-7 and 9-8 incorporate many attributes of the elements of dance. Both emphasize the dance element *time*. For younger students (Activity 9-7), differences in *tempo* are important. They travel in *general space* and use larger and smaller steps. Older students (Activity 9-8), experience *tempo, rhythm, pulse, syncopation* and *duration* as attributes of the element of time. Also for older students *body parts* are accentuated during the warm-up stretches and the gestures during skill reinforcements. Different *levels* of the body, body *shapes*, variations in *directions* and *pathways* are used throughout the lesson. Variations in *energy* expenditure are integrated into the culminating activity.

Activity 9-9
FULL LESSON PLAN
DANCING ADJECTIVES AND ADVERBS
ENERGY

Age:
3rd grade/older
Time:
  20 minutes

Music:
Several selections with different qualities and tempos, no lyrics
Materials:
A length of rope for tug-of-war
Objectives:
To explore contrasting movement qualities. To use adverbs and adjectives to relate to the dance element energy.

Warm-up/Introduction

1. Introduce/remind students of the dance element *energy*, and resulting movement qualities. (example: Strong, light; sudden, sustained; direct, indirect; bound, free flow. Chapter 3, page 17.)
2. In personal space students lazily perform a variation of stretches from Activity 9-8. (example: The first section, counting sixteen counts for each leg position.)
3. Reach for the ceiling, slowly roll the head and upper body down to a position hanging from waist.
4. Flatten the back parallel to the floor, arms out to the sides.
5. Curve back, arms alongside body, bending knees.
6. Slowly straighten legs as body rolls up to a standing position.
7. Repeat. Perform using little energy expenditure.
8. Ask students to describe the quality of the movement. (example: Slow, relaxing, boring, mushy, gluey, droopy.)

Then

9. Select two volunteers about the same size and weight to demonstrate.
10. Students hold a rope between them and enact a tug-of-war.
11. When they are about to pull each other over, call "freeze."
12. Ask the class to identify what parts of the body are being used.
13. Have the students describe the energy expenditure. (example: Is the action strong [tough] or light [wimpy]? Direct [nonstop] or indirect [roundabout]? Sustained [endless] or sudden [surprise]? Bound [tight] or free [loose] flow?)
14. Describe what the demonstrators are doing with their feet (versus their arms). (example: Pushing versus pulling.)

Activity 9-9, continued

15. Are they pulling and pushing as hard as they can?
16. Use adjectives to compare the movement quality of this activity with the warm-up.

Skill Reinforcement/Review

1. Place students in columns to move across the floor one row at a time.
2. Picture a large, heavy object, its size and shape. Ask several students to describe their object. (example: Refrigerator, box of books, oak dresser, old car.)
3. Students mime pushing the object (no wheels) across the floor, using different body parts. (example: Head, hip, foot, shoulder.)
4. Play slow, sustained music as students move across the floor, using different body parts.
5. Ask students to describe the energy expenditure/movement quality. (example: Strong [fierce], direct [straight], sustained [forever], bound [tense].)
   Then
6. Students cross the room, keeping an imaginary feather or balloon afloat, using different body parts.
7. Use lighter, faster, syncopated music.
8. Ask students to describe the energy used. (example: Light [wispy], indirect [uncontrollable], sudden [quick], free [flowing].)
   Then
9. Inform students that their teacher's desk (imaginary) is across the room.
10. They cross to the teacher's desk to tell the teacher that they have just cheated on the exam.
11. Discuss energy expenditure/quality of movement. (example: Generally light [weak], indirect [wimpy], sustained [not stopping], bound [rigid].)
    Then
12. Inform students that a loud speaker announcement will ask them to report to the principal's office.
13. They cross to the office immediately to claim their lottery winnings.
14. Discuss energy expenditure/quality of movement. (example: Strong [push], direct [go!], sudden [lightning], bound [stiff].)
    Then
15. Students work as partners.
16. Student in front is a kite and student in back is holding onto the kite string.
17. First the weather is nice with a light breeze, the person holding the string guides the kite.
18. A strong gust of wind catches the kite, and the out-of-control kite now controls the person.
19. Discuss the two contrasting qualities of movement. (example: Light, indirect [or direct], sustained, free; then strong, direct [or indirect], sudden, bound.)

Activity 9-9, continued

Culminating Activity/Students Apply the Lesson

1. Students are placed around the room in general space.
2. Students move as several images using contrasting movement qualities. (examples: Trunk of a palm tree swaying slightly side to side in a soft breeze, thin knife slashing through tall weeds, large bird hovering in the sky, making the bed—pulling the covers tight and fluffing the pillow, dripping wet beach towel wringing itself, sprinkling water on a shirt, stretching it out and ironing it dry, cutting an orange in half and squeezing out all its juice, angry monkey swatting a pesky fly darting around its head, cat waking up, stretching and pouncing on a ball, rock hammer rapidly chipping rocks, feet walking backward through sticky glue.)
3. Repeat and challenge students to be aware of differences in their energy expenditure and the resulting quality of the movement.
4. Place students in columns. Play background music as students perform, one row at a time.
5. Each student chooses and performs six of the images to move across the floor.
6. Freeze in the sixth image until everyone has finished. Use your peripheral vision to look for varying movement qualities.

Cool-down/Closure/Reflection

1. With everyone in personal space, discuss the images.
2. Describe variations in the energy expenditure and resulting movement qualities of each one. (example: Which felt most comfortable, which the least comfortable, which movement qualities did you like the best? Use energy attributes.)
3. Students create their own images demonstrating contrasting movement qualities.
4. They can use these for another dance activity at a later date or to write a story or poem.

Learning Outcomes:

Students expand movement and verbal vocabularies by using adverbs and adjectives to describe and create differing qualities in their movements. They relate attributes of the dance element energy to everyday activities.

Activity 9-9 emphasizes variations in the dance element *energy* and the resulting qualities of movement. It also stresses different parts of the *body* during the warm-up and skill reinforcement activities. Spatial awareness is evident during the skill reinforcements as students travel across the room changing *levels*, following different *directions* and *pathways*. *Rhythm* and *tempo* are influenced by the music used as well as being a result of individual movement choices. *Syncopation* is also present during sudden movements. Variations and contrasts of the dance element *energy* are present throughout, ranging from *strong* to *light*, *sudden* to *sustained*, *direct* to *indirect*, and *bound* to *free* movements.

Suggested lesson variations involving energy expenditure and resulting qualities of movement might include exploring natural phenomena such as volcanoes, tornados, earthquakes, or hurricanes.

There is no limit to the variations in scenarios that can be developed for age appropriate creative dance lessons. These lessons, by encouraging students to use descriptive adjectives and adverbs, enhance and expand both verbal and movement vocabularies at the same time that creative thinking skills are nurtured.

When creating new dance lesson plans, teachers need to consider variation possibilities for all four elements: *space, time, energy,* and *body* (see pages 15–17 to review these elements). One needs to continually ask oneself how attributes of each can be included. It is essential to add this focus to the lesson plan—which also encompasses strong objectives and learning outcomes, common grounds for students, and provide opportunities for all students to contribute creative and critical thinking skills.

> *I want my students to have the confidence to try new things*
> *and to not be afraid of doing something wrong.*
> *Second grade teacher*

Note for Chapter 9

1. Sometimes dance sessions in the classroom may involve little or no physical movement. Viewing a film or video dance presentation and discussing it using dance terminology may be the focus of the lesson.

TEN

The Teacher as Facilitator

I love creating lesson plans and working with younger children, but I learned that I must be detailed and clear with instructions when it comes to teaching and that a beautiful lesson plan without control measures and strategies to engage would be nothing. How to teach is just as important as what to teach.

> *Kindergarten teacher*

Teaching a lesson begins with creating a good lesson plan, but to actualize that lesson's content, teachers and students must perform it. Teachers are facilitators of that process. They must be seen, heard, and understood by their students. How teachers communicate their lessons evolves into their individual teaching style which distinguishes one teacher from another. However, a teacher's ultimate objective is not to entertain students as much as it is to stimulate their learning through modeling, clarification of concepts, and completing tasks. Therefore, viewing teachers as facilitators of learning involves identifying individual teaching styles as well as examining the methodology used to connect students with the lesson at hand.

Individual Teaching Style

An individual teaching style that evolves from implementing lesson plans is distinct from the content of the lesson itself. Personality features that students recognize in their teachers contribute significantly to the development of individual teaching style. When a group of student teachers[1] was asked to identify qualities they valued most in teachers and that they would like to personify themselves, they agreed upon the following, which fall into three patterns:

Those visibly first apparent in the teacher's performance:

- Enthusiastic, energetic, exciting.
- Fun, full of life.

147

Those recognized in performance over time:

- Knowledgeable, thoughtful.

- Creative, versatile.

- Organized, prepared, good time manager.

- In control, tough but fair.

- Great role model.

- Caring, cares about me, compassionate.

- Kind, helpful, warm.

- Easy to talk to.

Those based on experience:

- Willing to listen, pays attention.

- Encouraging, patient, understanding.

In a study that asked dance students in a public school to describe their feelings about dance class and their dance teachers, the majority stated that they especially enjoyed their dance classes, in contrast with other classes, because the teacher was more caring, more interested in them individually, and allowed them to be creative.[2]

Teaching Methodology to Engage and Direct/Control Learning

Teaching styles include strategies to motivate students and also parameters or control measures. Initially, strategies to engage are helpful when some students, fearing unfamiliar activities, may be resistant to dancing. They will need encouragement to try something new. Control measures become particularly relevant for teachers in dance activity classes because students are physically moving about the space.

Engagement strategies and control measures help avoid confusion and conflict, which may result in unsuccessful completion of activities, when time should be spent on developing skills.

Procedural Choices to Engage Students

Create a pleasant, enjoyable atmosphere. Most agree that successful learning occurs in a pleasant, relatively stress-free environment. This does not mean that students are left unchallenged. Rather, it implies that attaining greater heights in learning is something pleasurable to achieve. When students refer to having fun, they rarely mean that what they are doing is unimportant or not serious to them. To the contrary, a "fun" situation means that students want to do the activity, they feel challenged by it, and can expect to be treated with respect. Therefore, creating an enjoyable atmosphere affords teachers opportunities to engage students in learning.

Establish familiar common ground to begin. Part of making learning enjoyable is to begin on common ground and progress from there. The use of imagery and recalling familiar items and behaviors in designing and implementing dance lessons is an important aspect of establishing a common ground for students.

Provide opportunity for students to contribute creatively. Teachers use improvisation, guided discovery, and problem solving as procedures to encourage and validate students' choices. This occurs first with young children by asking them specific questions to encourage single choices and then later more complex choices. With older students, strategies used to engage them creatively are improvisation, responding quickly to various stimuli, guided discovery, exploring suggested variations of movements, and problem solving—creating a dance utilizing several stated parameters.

Assure students that everyone will have a turn. For all ages, it is important that they know they will each have a turn, and that they will be expected to be a part of the activity. In school dance classes participation is not dependent on who is the loudest, always in front, or the best dancer. Everyone contributes to the activity. When it is impossible for each student to have a turn playing the drum on a given day, for instance, keep a record so that each student will have the opportunity at some point.

Arrange productive groupings of students. Consider the best group arrangement for specific classes. For instance, some students will get lost in one large group and not feel a part of the activity, and other students will be uncomfortable working alone. Working in partners or small groups helps many students feel more at ease. Select age appropriate groupings. Preschool children work best one-on-one with the teacher or in a large circle moving together. Kindergarten- through second-grade children are usually ready to begin working with partners. Upper elementary and older students are ready to problem solve cooperatively in small groups. When selecting students for each group, use numbering systems or other random descriptive criteria—everyone wearing blue, or everyone whose name begins with an A—to assure students that they will all be placed in a group, that they do not have to worry about other classmates choosing or not choosing them.

Afford different leading and following positions for students. As discussed in Chapter 6, teachers can choose different leading techniques to engage students: students shadow (perform behind the teacher), students echo (repeat after the teacher), teacher mirrors students (faces students using opposite side of students), or call and response (students create own response to teacher's action). Teachers may also have students exchange roles with each other, some teaching other students a new activity and then reversing roles. Using alphabetical order or another class specific system, students can assume leadership roles for movement activities like locomotor movements across the room. Again, it is important to make clear that each student will have the chance to lead at some time.

Use hands-on related objects when applicable. Students are involved when asked to play the drum or other instrument to accompany the class's movement, to count vertebrae on a model skeleton when studying movement of the spine, to use scarves to move like the wind, or to blow up a balloon to practice expanding and contracting movement. Creating lessons that can utilize applicable physical hands-on objects engages many otherwise hesitant students. Appendices A-1 through A-4 and A-20 suggest possibilities for hands-on props for specific activities and lessons in this text.

Procedural Choices to Direct or Control Learning

Provide specific instructions. Successful lessons begin with clear specific instructions and stated rules of expected behavior. Teachers must have a picture in their own minds of what they will ask students to do and what the desired learning outcomes are. Specific instructions do not inhibit students' creative contribution. Instead, they clarify given parameters to solve the movement problem and identify other details that students must create.

Students might be asked to travel forward quickly in sixteen counts, create a sixteen count movement phrase in personal space, and then during thirty-two counts return slowly to the opening position. Within that stated structure of sixty-four counts, the student creates the specific movements for each segment.

Make clear the consequences for not following rules. At the beginning of each activity state rules for participation and consequences when those rules are not followed. For example, when it is a student's turn to be leader of a particular exercise, the student must follow the leadership rules: listen, follow instructions, and be ready to lead the activity. If the student starts talking to another student or in any way disrupts the class, the leadership role is relinquished. Be prepared to enforce rules, so do not make those that can not be enforced. Following rules helps establish a sense of cooperative and fair play.

Establish clear beginning and ending cues. When students will be moving around the room, it is essential they know when to begin and to end moving. You may ask students to spread out around the room, to move freely to the music the way it makes them feel. But you ask them to move only when they hear the music, to freeze when it is silent, to move within a designated area, and not to bump into anyone else. It is also important that students begin and end moving at specified times so they do not experience false starts with the music. This is particularly true for students who are unsure of a dancing activity. They need the security of beginning together. Therefore it is helpful to establish a certain number of counts before they begin moving. For example count, beat, or clap four counts (1, 2, 3, 4 or 5, 6, 7, 8) and everyone begins together on the next count. The teacher or student leader needs to give that instruction very clearly.

Establish clear beginning and ending placement. In addition to understanding when to begin and end movements, students need to know where in the designated space to begin and end. Are they sitting or standing, and what is their spatial relationship with other students? It is important to stress that most dance activities should begin and end in personal space. In other words instruct students to find personal space at the beginning and the end of each activity (see Activities 4–18, page 43, and 4–27, page 52) and to maintain space between themselves and others throughout activities. When students are brainstorming and solving movement problems as groups, it is helpful for them to sit when they have finished. The teacher can then see when everyone is ready to receive instructions for the next step.

Check students' understanding of instructions. After giving instructions, ask questions about the instructions or have students repeat instructions to make sure everyone is listening and knows what to do. Sometimes, especially with young children, students will be so excited about dancing that they completely forget what exactly they are supposed to do when the music or the specific activity begins.

Model desired behavior. Teachers may choose to model individual activities themselves or ask individual students, partners, or a smaller group to demonstrate movements before everyone tries the activity. This affords control by clarifying what is about to occur.

Arrange productive groupings of students. Before an activity begins decide the group formation—partners, small groups, one large group, individual—that will work best to introduce, learn, and perform the activity. Predetermining group composition (rather than letting students choose their own) and what form of random selection to use is also a control measure, as well as a strategy to engage, is discussed earlier. It controls by separating friends and students who always work together and therefore may choose to socialize rather than concentrate on completing the task at hand. (As an engagement strategy it also assures less assertive students that they will be placed in a group.)

When students feel a sense of structure that control measures provide, they feel safe in the learning environment and are motivated to participate and perform their best.

Following are suggestions of specific instructions and actions teachers can use during "moving" activities to continue student engagement and to maintain parameters within which all can successfully create together.

Using the Elements of Dance to Engage and Control

Body

Use body parts when giving instructions:

- "All noses looking at me" (facing the teacher).
- "Eyes on the sides and back of your head" (avoids bumping into others).
- "Quiet feet beneath you on the floor" (stop moving).

- Raise your hand or other designated body part (to mean silence).

Provide stick figure drawings illustrating body contour, body parts used.[3]

Space

Using personal space

- Students "sit during instructions" (the teacher see everyone, and it is easier to maintain control).
- Students "sit when finished" (know everyone is finished, and it is easier to give next instruction).
- Students "find personal space at the beginning and ending of activities" (control movement).

Using general space

- "Look for space where no one else is; use all the corners" (avoid crowding).
- Tap on student's shoulder when to begin and end (to limit number entering or leaving space at one time).
- Place students in columns, one row at time (to control how many move at once, making sure everyone has a turn).
- Place in circle (to see everyone at once).
- Placement of teacher (in front, with back to students; students shadow and move to the same side).
- Placement of teacher (facing students, mirror their movements; he or she can see everyone).
- Placement of teacher (next to a specific student; provides needed help or control).
- Change front of the room (students in the back now in front; keeps students alert).
- Placement of students (change place in lines or room; everyone has a chance to be leader).
- Designate the space to be used with cones or other physical designations (controls area used).

Time

Using sound accompaniment

- Music with no lyrics (engages creativity without following specifi words).

- Music from other countries and of various styles (brings about variety in music experience).

- Sound effects (establishes a familiar environment).

Using instruments

- Controls beginning, ending, tempo, rhythm of activity.

- Provides pulse for activity.

- Engages students using the instruments to accompany activities; to follow or choose tempo, rhythm, duration (Students accompanying do not dance, they remain stationary).

- Students practice listening skills.

- Students follow rhythm by clapping, snapping or stamping.

Activity structure

- Count designated counts before beginning so students will begin together (example: four counts for nothing, 5, 6, 7, 8 begin).

- In the canon form, students begin the same movement at specified intervals (example: At every four counts the next row begins).

- Improvisation (students perform spontaneously, taking no time to plan responses).

- Reflection (take time to wait for answers during performance discussion).

- Duration (designate an amount of time for problem-solving and presentation).

Energy

- Pacing of class (vary energy cues to calm down and to enliven as needed).

- End activity quietly (slow activity pace and use quiet voice).
(example: The plane lands and gradually slows down on the runway.)

- Imagery (stimulate energy variations in movement qualities).
  (example: The balloon sways gently.)

Imagery is a valuable strategy for engaging students. It expands both move- **Imagery**
ment and verbal vocabulary. Encourage students to use descriptive adjectives and
adverbs when describing the quality of a movement. Encourage students to create
their own images, but in the beginning they will benefit from receiving detailed
images from the teacher to enhance their movement performance.

A good image will incorporate attributes from at least two elements of dance:

- Example: Move like popcorn popping.
  Better: Move like popcorn popping fast (time, tempo) in all directions
  (space, direction).
- Example: Bird flying.
- Better: The bird circled (space, pathway) slowly (time, tempo) in the sky.
- Example: The eagle caught its prey.
  Better: The eagle swooped (energy, strong sudden) down (space, level)
  and grabbed (energy, sudden) its prey.
- Example: The frog jumped to a lily pad.
  Better: The frog jumped quickly (time, tempo) from one lily pad
  across (space) to another.

Images engage students and suggest shades and nuances of meaning. They
help students and teachers define the activity and begin to consider multiple variations and possibilities in their dances. In this way both teachers and students begin
to feel comfortable performing the movement and expanding their movement
experience. Embellishing images with music or sound accompaniment and visuals
further engages interest and creativity. The ultimate goal for all of these engagement
strategies is that students will begin providing their own image details.

> *The most important thing I've learned is to not be afraid to open myself
> when teaching and performing. It brings much more to the classroom when
> you are enjoying yourself.*
>
> *Fourth grade teacher*

Notes for Chapter 10

1. These comments were the combined results from several years (1995-2004) of questioning students in a class called "Creative Dance for Children" for pre-service education majors at California State University in Fullerton.

2. Stinson, "Meaning and Value: Reflections on What Students Say about School." Additional research regarding student feelings about teachers can be found in the Research in Dance Education database (www.ndeo.org/research). Begin with "education issue" category: affective domain, and "area of service" categories: teacher preparation and pedagogy.

3. I started using stick figure drawings (like the ones used in this text to illustrate activities) in dance classes when I was teaching at a school for dyslexic and learning disabled students. I found that being able to see the shape or contour of the body in a stick figure was helpful for many students who had a weak sense of body image. Also, a series of illustrations for one exercise helped students remember the sequence.

ELEVEN

Assessment

*I learned that closing the lesson is important. The wrap-up questions allow
the student to calm down and for the teacher to check for understanding. This
is important because the teacher may have to do another lesson depending on
the students' knowledge. Closing the lesson is also important to tie in an
extended arts project.*

> *First grade teacher*

Assessing students' learning and progress has always been part of a teacher's
responsibility. These tasks involve linking assessment to learning and to teaching,
advancing student learning and improving teaching environments, identifying what
exactly is assessable, and determining how to document learning as part of assessment. Dance educators have contributed to ongoing assessment discussions. For
example, Marcia Lloyd has summarized the evolution in thinking about dance
assessment over the years.[1] Anne Green Gilbert has prepared personal-assessment
question forms for both students and teachers,[2] and Theresa Purcell Cone has
designed examples for assessing dance in elementary physical education.[3]

Assessing Dance Activities

Generally, procedures used to assess dance learning in school reflect current
methodology centered on "performance based" assessment.[4] All forms of assessment
should evaluate and document student and teacher performance, how students and
teachers go about accomplishing their tasks as well as task completion. Ideally, performance-based assessment should imply more than passing a particular achievement or aptitude test. It should refer to the process of applying knowledge and
demonstrating understanding. This might be a teacher explaining a new concept to
a class, a student dancing a creative dance sequence, or a class as a whole working
on a project.

Assessment should be student-centered, involving students in the process; standards-based, enforcing established content and achievement expectations; and constructive, aiming at continuing improvement.

"Authentic assessment" is another term used to identify reliable or trustworthy performance. Assessment is authentic when it is evaluating a performance that is particularly meaningful to the participant and demonstrates a broad application of knowledge[5]. Student-produced portfolios, journals, models, arts expressions including live performances, and other hands-on activities documenting student learning could be considered authentic assessments.[6]

Using pre-established criteria, authentic assessment procedures can assess both subjective and objective aspects of dance activities. This methodology encourages teachers and students to respect the time they invest in contemplating, interpreting, and responding to learning. These procedures develop insights that potentially connect learning achievement across the curriculum, not just during art making process activities.

Standards–Based Pre-established Criteria

Standards for Dance in Early Childhood, National Standards for Arts Education, and the National Standards for Dance Education cited earlier (see Appendix B–1) specify movement and motor skills that students should be able to perform at specific ages. They also provide guidelines for other arts knowledge that students should be able to demonstratively understand and apply. By following criteria defined in these standards teachers can observe and assess students' achievement of fundamental motor skills, knowledge, and understanding.

Standards for Dance in Early Childhood also provides a rubric for assessing student performance: "needs improvement," "meets the standard," and "outstanding." Using this rubric, preschool and elementary school teachers can fairly objectively assess students' performance. However, all evaluations made by a student's teacher (as opposed to an outside adjudicator) will be subjective in the sense that the teacher and student know where exactly the student began trying to learn, how much improvement has occurred, and how much time it took.

Additional Pre-established Criteria

Before activities and lessons begin, teachers and students define together additional pre-established assessment criteria as needed. Examples of such criteria could involve student performance behavior as they observe, create, perform, and reflect during dance sessions.

Observing **involves students behaving appropriately:** paying attention, watching, listening, and appreciating.

Creating **involves students participating fully:** respecting established rules/parameters, expending effort whether quietly contemplating or physically moving, trying to be original while constructing variations for the stated problem, totally concentrating on the work at hand, and respecting group members' contributions.

Performing **involves students focusing on the presentation of the creation:** conscientiously demonstrating what was created, being prepared by knowing what is happening (and having rehearsed if appropriate), expending enthusiastic effort, demonstrating ongoing concern with the form the presentation takes and how it looks, and respecting group members' performances.

Reflecting **involves students contemplating fully what is being planned or has just occurred:** asking questions, answering questions posed, comparing and contrasting with other expressions, imagining variations, examining personal responses.

Within these general criteria, specific details of individual performance can be noted to quantify achieved learning and demonstrated understanding. These might include such points as whether or not a specific dance skill has been learned, if requested elements of dance were recognized and utilized in solving a movement problem, or if a relevant dance has been recalled and contrasted, or if students respect or appreciate the efforts of their classmates. It is important to always remember that assessment of degrees of excellence in dance skill performance is not a primary objective of dance activities in preschool and elementary school settings.

Reflection as On-Going Assessment

Taking time to reflect on activities is an important aspect of assessment. Reflection, which incorporates honing observation ability, is a skill that needs to be introduced, encouraged, and nurtured for both students and teachers.

By taking class time to prepare for and to reflect about an activity, teachers can influence students' attitudes about, understanding of, and appreciation for assessment procedures in general.

When students and teachers plan an activity together, reflection questions following the presentation may be pre-established by the class or developed from the National Standards criteria previously mentioned. Questions can be both objective and subjective.

Objective questions during reflection of a dance activity[7] might include the following:

- Did the activity satisfy the requirements of the assignment given?
- Did it provide a solution to the problem posed?
- Was the solution original, something not seen before in the class?
- How were the elements of dance, *body, space, time,* and *energy,* used?
- Were there variations in the movements or was there sameness throughout?
- How did the variations or sameness influence the final outcome?
- Were the movements and/or dance steps familiar?
- What variations in the movements or elements of dance could be used?
- How did the group work together? Was everyone involved?

These questions can be altered to accommodate different age groups. For example, objective questions for a kindergarten or pre-school class might include the following:

- What parts of the body moved?
- Did they move quickly or slowly?
- Can you think of other body parts that could be used?
- Did the dancers use personal or general space?
- Did the dancers dance in a group, with partners, or alone?

Subjective questions regarding personal feelings and opinions about the performance might include the following:

- What about the dance did you especially like?
- Why do you think you liked that?
- How did you feel when you were watching (or dancing)? Did you enjoy it?
- How do you think the dancers (or audience) were feeling?
- What do you think the choreographer was trying to say?
- Describe what you saw or heard that makes you think and feel that way.
- Did the dance remind you of anything you have ever seen?
- Does the dance give you any ideas for a dance you might create?

How well and to what depth students answer subjective questions comprises part of an ultimate letter or number evaluation. Subjective assessment can also reflect observable change and growth witnessed in students' subsequent performances as documented in their own self-evaluation and stated goals.

Reflection assessment questions above concerned valuing group dance activities as creative expression. Although such reflection involved observing performances of their classmates, students were not asked to assess (or grade) individual student performances of the activity.[8] But students' involvement with their own learning progress is an important part of authentic performance-based assessment.

Student Self-Reflection and Performance Assessment

Student assessment of their individual dance experience can be documented via a variety of age-appropriate expressive outlets:

- Students keep daily journals describing what they personally experienced and learned.
- Students write letters to the teacher sharing feelings about their own performance of specific assignments, listing future goals for self-improvement, and evaluating their performances accordingly.
- Students draw pictures of themselves dancing movements they performed and showing how they felt while dancing.
- Students write essays reflecting on their group experience and describing their specific part in the group expression.

Students discussing their performance one-on-one with teachers can address the following:

- Were the requirements of the assignment satisfied?
- Was the student prepared to perform?
- Did the student participate fully? Know the movements or procedure that was determining the movement sequence?
- Was the student following the rhythm and/or keeping the tempo of the music?
- How did the student move in terms of space used and energy applied?
- Were variations in the elements of dance employed?
- Comparison with previous performances and observed growth.
- Prepare a checklist for desired future improvement.

Students add to their learning and understanding as part of their participation in authentic performance-based assessment rather than end their learning with a culminating grade. Unlike many traditional forms of assessment, authentic performance-based assessment addresses ongoing process and future potential. It requires that possibility be recognized, explored, and valued at all times during the procedure.

Assessment becomes part of the learning process with both teachers and students participating.

Students may be asked to define appropriate criteria upon which to be evaluated. They can create parts of the "test" and designate appropriate solutions. Examining what students feel they should be achieving and experiencing provides teachers with valuable insights about student learning. At the same time, students gain new understanding about their own capabilities instead of fearing assessment procedures.

Teacher Self-Reflection and Performance Assessment

Knowledge gained from self-reflection helps teachers refine their teaching performance, revise lesson planning, and develop new criteria for evaluating students.[9]

A teacher's self-reflection following a dance activity may include:

- Did the theme, time of day, or place of the lesson affect its outcome?

- Identify feelings before, during, and following the lesson.

- What worked especially well? What not so well?

- Were lesson objectives met? Did students demonstrate expected learning outcomes?

- Did all students participate? Were they challenged? Were they confused?

- Describe students' overall reaction and response. Was it a surprise?

- How well did you incorporate the elements of dance and their variations?

- Did the lesson ask for variety in locomotor and non-locomotor movements?

- Was creativity encouraged? Were students individually creative or copying each other?

- How well did students participate during reflection?

- How effective were your strategies to engage and control students?

- What did you learn from teaching this lesson?

- Would you repeat this lesson? What would you change? How might you develop it further?

Recommending Outside Dance Training for Students

This book has focused on dancing in preschools and elementary schools. It has discussed the objectives of dance education and its benefits for students in such settings. Nurturing specialized dance technique and performance skills is not one of those objectives. However, school teachers are in the unique position to observe their students' responses to dancing activity, and in the best interests of their students, they may observe some who would benefit from focused training in a dance studio outside of school.

There are many reasons to recommend specialized dance training for students, both boys and girls. Most people immediately think of the student (most often a girl) who moves easily without visible effort, who seemingly hears music more precisely than others, who is unusually creative, and/or who enthusiastically shares his/her passion for dancing with the teacher. Teachers may feel that such a student must have a special talent that should be nurtured and developed. That should not be overlooked.

There are many other young people whose lives could be greatly enhanced with dance training. These may include a child who has difficulty mastering fundamental motor skills, a child who is generally awkward and clumsy, a child who is overweight, a child who is shy and withdrawn, a child who has difficulty being assertive in group activities, a child with limited verbal expression (for whatever reason, including a child who does not speak English well), a child who has difficulty moving expansively in large spaces, a child who cannot keep from touching everything in sight and cannot maintain personal space, a child with visual and/or auditory impairments, or a child who is intimidated by competitive athletics.[10]

Every dance school director has many stories of children who came to them with varying physical, emotional, and social difficulties; and who through dance classes developed a sense of self and went on to achieve success in school and life. If you have any students who might benefit from dance training, it could be very important for that student to investigate a dance school that will be able to help him or her achieve success. Speaking with the school director will usually tell a great deal about whether or not that school will be able to assist the student in question. Perhaps you have an ongoing relationship with a local dance school that could help. If not, Appendix C-2 provides a resource for locating an outside-of-school dance program.

I like to dance because it makes me feel good inside
and it makes me feel full of joy.
   Student, eight years old

Notes for Chapter 11

1. Lloyd, *Adventures in Creative Movement Activities: A Guide to Teaching,* pp. 215-231.

2. Gilbert, *Creative Dance for All Ages,* pp. 341-349.

3. Purcell Cone, *Assessing Dance in Elementary Physical Education.*

4. Schmid, "Authentic Assessment in the Arts: A Web-based Design for Benchmarking of State and National Standards," p. 32. Dance educator Dale Schmid identifies performance assessment as assessing students "on both the process and end result of their work." He further contrasts alternative (performance assessment) with traditional forms of assessment as opportunities for students "to create a response to a question or task," rather than "choose a response from a given list."

5. Ibid., p. 33. Schmid defines an authentic task as one "designed to elicit from students their application of a broad range of knowledge and skills to solve a complex problem."

6. Lazaroff, "Performance and Motivation in Dance Education," p. 23, makes these connections.

7. Objective questions developed by pre-service education students participating in the university dance course titled "Creative Dance for Children" at California State University at Fullerton, 1995-2004. Regardless of students' ages, answers to these objective questions can all be factually based on what students and teachers observed during the activity. Ultimately, when needed, number or letter grades for individual performances can be based on values placed on applicable factual questions: how important was it to follow the outline of the assignment? What were the different parts of that outline, and out of a possible 100 points how much is fulfilling each part worth?

8. See Note 2 above.

9. For guidelines for teachers' self-assessment in arts activities see *Interstate New Teacher Assessment and Support Consortium, Model Standards for Licensing Classroom Teachers and Specialists in the Arts: A Resource for State Dialogue.* Also available at http://www.ccsso.org/intasc.html.

10. Elsa Posey, RDE and Director, Posey School of Dance, Northport, NY, contributed greatly to this list via email communication dated January 28, 2005.

Bibliography of References

Arts Education Partnership. (2002). *Critical Links: Learning in the Arts and Student Academic and Social Development.* Edited by Richard J. Deasy. Washington, D.C.: Arts Education Partnership.

Ashton–Warner, Sylvia. (1963). *Teacher.* New York: Simon and Schuster.

Bateson, Gregory. (1972). "A Theory of Play and Fantasy." In *Steps to an Ecology of Mind: Collected Essays in Anthropology, Psychiatry, Evolution, and Epistemology.* San Francisco: Chandler Publishing Co.

Blacking, John. (1985). "Movement, Dance, Music, and the Venda Girls' Initiation Cycle." In *Society and the Dance: The Social Anthropology of Process and Performance.* Edited by Paul Spencer. Cambridge, England: Cambridge University Press.

Bonbright, Jane. (2001). "National Support of Arts Education: Linking Dance to Arts Education Reform." In *Journal of Dance Education,* 1, no.1: 7-13.

Caillois, Roger. (1958). *Man, Play, and Games.* Translated by Meyer Barash. New York: The Free Press of Glencoe.

California Department of Education. (1996). *Visual and Performing Arts Framework for California Public Schools.* Sacramento, CA: California State Department of Education.

Cone, Theresa Purcell. (2005) *Assessing Dance in Elementary Physical Education.* Reston, VA: AAHPERD.

Consortium of National Arts Education Associations. (1994) *National Standards for Arts Education: Dance, Music, Theatre, and Visual Arts.* Reston, VA: AAHPERD.

Corso, Marjorie. (1997). "Children Who Desperately Want to Read, but Are Not Working at Grade Level: Use Movement Patterns as "Windows" to Discover Why." ERIC Document ED402549: pp. 1-27.

_____. (1999). "Children Who Desperately Want to Read, but Are Not Working at Grade Level: Use Movement Patterns as "Windows" to Discover Why." Part II: The Transverse Midline. ERIC Document ED432733: pp. 1-17.

_____. (1999). "Children Who Desperately Want to Read, but Are Not Working at Grade Level: Use Movement Patterns as "Windows" to Discover Why." Part III: The Frontal Midline. ERIC Document ED432751: pp. 1-11.

_____. (1999). "Children Who Desperately Want to Read, but Are Not Working at Grade Level: Use Movement Patterns as "Windows" to Discover Why." Part IV: Crossing All

Three Midlines Automatically. ERIC Document ED432752: pp. 1–13.

Dunkin, Anne. (2004). "Gliding *Glissade* not *Grand Jeté*: Elementary Classroom Teachers Teaching Dance." In *Arts Education Policy Review,* 105, no.3: pp. 23–29.

Dunkin-Willis, Anne. (1979). "The Integrative Aspects of Structured Movement Activity in the Education of the Whole Child: Contributions of Edward Seguin, Rudolf Steiner, Emile Jaques-Dalcroze, and Rudolf Laban." M.A. thesis, University of Maryland.

Dunkin-Willis, Anne. (1998). "Marking Time and Space Together: An Interpretation of Young People's Dancing as Cultural Play." Ph.D. dissertation, University of California, Riverside.

Gardner, Howard. (1983). *Frames of Mind: The Theory of Multiple Intelligences.* New York: Basic Books.

Gardner, Howard. (2000). *Intelligence Reframed: Multiple Intelligences for the 21st Century.* New York: Basic Books.

Gilbert, Anne Green. (1996). *Creative Dance for All Ages.* Reston, VA: AAHPERD.

Huizinga, Johan. (1970). *Homo Ludens: A Study of the Play Element in Culture.* New York: Harper and Row.

Interstate New Teacher Assessment and Support Consortium. (2002). *Model Standards for Licensing Classroom Teachers and Specialists in the Arts: A Resource for State Dialogue.* Washington, DC: Council of Chief State School Officers.

Kraus, Richard, Sarah Chapman Hilsendager, and Brenda Dixon. (1991). *History of the Dance in Art and Education.* Englewood Cliffs, NJ: Prentice-Hall, Inc.

Laban, Rudolf. (1948). *Modern Educational Dance.* London: MacDonald and Evans.

Large, Elizabeth. (2005). "The Next Dance: Hit TV Show, Movies Fuel the Ballroom Craze." In *The Baltimore Sun.* July 17, 2005: N1, N6.

Lazaroff, Elizabeth. (2001). "Performance and Motivation in Dance Education." In *Arts Education Policy Review.* 103, no. 2: pp. 23–29.

Lerch, Harold A., John E. Becker, and Bonnie M. Ward. (1974). *Perceptual-Motor Learning: Theory and Practice.* Palo Alto, CA: Peek Publications.

Lloyd, Marcia L. (1998) *Adventures in Creative Movement Activities: A Guide for Teaching.* Dubuque, Iowa: Eddie Bowers Publishing, Inc.

Mead, Margaret. (1939). "Coming of Age in Samoa." In *From the South Seas; Studies of Adolescence and Sex in Primitive Societies.* New York: William Morrow and Co.

Milhollan, Frank, and Bill Forisha. (1972). *From Skinner to Rogers: Contrasting Approaches to Education.* Lincoln, NE: Professional Educators Publications, Inc.

National Association for Sport and Physical Education. (2004). *Moving into the Future: National Standards for Physical Education.* (2nd Edition). Reston, VA: NASPE.

National Center for Education Statistics (NCES), Office of Educational Research and Improvement. (2002). *Arts Education in Public Elementary and Secondary Schools: 1999-2000.* Washington, DC: U.S. Department of Education.

National Dance Association. (1994). *National Standards for Dance Education: What Every Young American Should Know and Be Able to Do in Dance.* Reston, VA: AAHPERD.

National Dance Association. (1995). *National Standards for Dance Education Plus the Opportunity-to-Learn Standards for Dance Education* (2nd edition). Reston, VA: AAHPERD.

National Dance Association. (1997). *National Standards for Dance Education plus the Opportunity-to-Learn Standards for Dance Education* (3rd edition). Reston, VA: AAHPERD.

National Dance Education Organization. (2003). *Standards for Dance in Early Childhood.* (Draft). Bethesda, MD: NDEO.

National Dance Education Organization. (2004). *Research Priorities for Dance Education: A Report to the Nation.* Bethesda, MD: NDEO.

National Dance Education Organization. (2005). *Standards for Dance Learning and Teaching in the Arts: Ages 5-18.* Bethesda, MD: NDEO.

National Dance Education Organization. (2005). *Professional Teaching Standards for Dance in Arts Education.* Bethesda, MD: NDEO.

North, Marion. (1975). *Personality Assessment through Movement.* Boston: Plays, Inc.

Park, Clara C. (1997). "Learning Style Preferences of Asian American (Chinese, Korean, and Vietnamese) Students in Secondary Education." In *Equity and Excellence in Education,* 30, no. 2: 68-77.

Park, Clara C. (1997). "Learning Style Preferences of Korean-, Mexican-, Armenian-American and Anglo Students in Secondary Schools." In *NASSP Bulletin,* 81, no. 585: 103-11.

Park, Clara C. (2000). "Learning Style Preferences of Southeast Asian Students." In *Urban Education,* 35, no. 3: 245-68.

Rosaldo, Renato. (1989). *Culture and Truth: The Remaking of Social Analysis.* Boston: Beacon Press.

Rugg, Harold Ordway. (1963). *Imagination.* New York: Harper and Row.

Schmid, Dale. (2001). "Authentic Assessment in the Arts: A Web-based Design for Benchmarking of State and National Standards." M.Ed. thesis, Temple University.

Stinson, Susan W. (1993). "Meaning and Value: Reflections on What Students Say about School." In *Journal of Curriculum and Supervision,* 8, no.3: 16–38.

Tomko, Linda. (1999). *Dancing Class.* Bloomington, IN: Indiana University Press.

Turner, Victor. (1969). *The Ritual Process: Structure and Anti-structure.* Chicago: Aldine Publishing Co.

APPENDIX A

Equipment and Materials to Enhance Dance Activities

A-1 Most toy stores sell small skeletons. If a physical skeleton is not feasible, this drawing can be used to illustrate the different vertebrae.

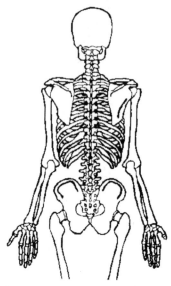

A-2 Strips of ribbon (30 inches long or so) placed on the floor can designate a river or mud puddle to assist students' learning to "leap" over or across it. Place the ribbons on the floor, parallel to each other, and then increase the distance between them as students become more comfortable leaping across. (I like to use blue, green, and white streamers to represent river colors.) Besides designating something to jump over, different colored streamers, ribbons, and scarves are useful for many creative dance exercises. They can emphasize flowing, spiraling, and lighter movement quality as well as represent specific choices of students. For example, they may become a cape or skirt, a scarf or veil, wings of a bird, mane of a pony, tail on an elephant, a tablecloth for a picnic, and any other things children create. These props are particularly nice because children will not be hurt if one hits them during the dance. (However, rules need to be established that they are not used to wrap around others or tie them up.) Girls all ages and younger boys (yes, boys) enjoy moving with these props and creating shapes and pathways with them in the air and on the floor. If scarves or ribbons are different colors, decide before handing them out what criteria you will use to determine who gets which color so that students will not keep requesting a different color from the one they receive.

A-3 Yarn balls are useful props for dance sessions, and they are relatively easy to make. Use different colors. Cut strips of yarn into six inch lengths (or a little longer) and tie a bunch of them together by wrapping yarn around the bunch four or five times. (A nice sized "bunch" is enough to fit in the space created by touching the tip of your middle finger to the tip of your thumb.) After bunches are tied, pull the opposite ends of the yarn toward each other until they form a ball shape and the ties in the middle are not visible. Yarn balls are good for clutching, throwing, catching, and any number of activities, and no one is hurt with yarn balls. If applicable for the activity, it is useful to have one color for right hand/foot movements and a contrasting color for left hand/foot movements.

A-4 Various sized hula hoops, depending on the age of students involved, are another useful prop for dance sessions. They can be employed for many activities as obstacles to go under, over, around, through; as props to simulate circular movement; or any other uses that students and teachers can create for them.

A-5 A video demonstrating a hip hop routine taught by young people titled *Hip Hop Kidz: Taught by Kids, Danced by Kids* is available from Princeton Book Company, 1-800-220-7149 or http://www.dancehorizons.com.

A-6 Instructional or viewing materials for ballroom dances are found in *Dancetime II: 500 Years of Social Dance Volume II: 20th Century,* available from Princeton Book Company, 1-800-220-7149 or http://www.dancehorizons.com.

A-7 There are two historical aspects to consider when planning this activity. The first addresses music accompaniment for the dance. Collections of Renaissance dance music available on CDs in most music stores usually include several *pavanes* (also spelled *pavan*). These will work well as accompaniment for this activity. Second, asking students to draw floor plans of symmetrical pathways for their dances illustrates an important feature of a form of dance notation first published in 1700 and used in printed dance manuals of the time. In that notation, called Feuillet notation, the dance's pathway is quite noticeable. However, on closer inspection you can also see markings indicating specific steps and their musical timing along the pathway. Dance students of the time learned how to read these various aspects of the notation as part of learning the dance. Examples of Feuillet notation (named for its author, Raoul Auger Feuillet) can be viewed using the following online search path/key words: Raoul Auger Feuillet > Dance Instruction Manuals, Baroque Dance Page Image Viewer > complete author/title list. Bypass the dance titles listed alphabetically to the authors' titles. Click on the first Feuillet citation in English and go to pages 101 to 120 to view several dances using Feuillet notation.

Please note that with respect to students creating a *pavane*, as described in Activity 7-3, the emphases on spatial configurations by drawing a floor plan, and performing the dance in a slow sustained manner are only a few features of court dancing of the time. Variations in the dance elements of time and energy were also very significant in seventeenth-century dances. Both slower sustained dances and lively quicker dances were popular. Much of the music composed at that time was written for specific dance rhythms, and a dancer's ability to perform the correct timing of the dances was just as important as their use of space. However, throughout the dances the vertical alignment and presence of the body along with symmetrical and harmonious movement were honored.

A-8 Except when noted otherwise, instructional notes, videos/DVDs, and music CDs for these dances listed in Activity 7-5 (and others as well) are included in *Favorite Folk Dances of Kids and Teachers* or *Multicultural Folk Dance Treasure Chest*. Both packages are available from Princeton Book Company, 1-800-220-7149 or http://www.dancehorizons.com.

A-9 Good introduction and instructional resource for African improvisational dances is found in *Favorite Folk Dances of Kids and Teachers*. Instructional notes, video/DVD, and music CD for **Bongo** is included in Volume 1 and for **Highlife** in Volume 3.

A-10 Visit www.whydidthechickencrosstheroad.com for **Chicken Dance** movement and music.

A-11 Information about **Haka** dance movements can be obtained by visiting: www.newzealand.com/travel/about-nz/culture/haka-feature/haka.cfm.

A-12 Instructional notes, video/DVD, and music CD for **Hora** are included in Favorite *Folk Dances of Kids and Teachers*, Volume 1.

A-13 Instructional notes, video/DVD, and music CD for **Huayno** are found in *Favorite Folk Dances of Kids and Teachers*, Volume 1.

A-14 **Hukilau** tells the story of attending a luau. Instructional notes, video/DVD and music CD are included in *Multicultural Folk Dance Treasure Chest*, Volume 1 (see Note A-8 above). **Aloha Kakahiaka,** a "good morning dance" is a short dance. Instructional notes, video/DVD, and music CD are included in *Favorite Folk Dances of Kids and Teachers*, Volume 3 (see Note A-8 above).

A-15 Instructional notes, video/DVD, and music CD for **La Raspa** are found in *Favorite Folk Dances of Kids and Teachers*, Volume 4. Included are both a novelty version and a traditional version.

A-16 *Authentic Indian Dances and Folklore* contains **Rain Dance** and is available through Educational Record Center, 1-888-372-4543 or http://www.erckids.com. The package includes a cassette and guide that describes fundamental Native American dance steps and provides drumming and chanting accompaniment.

A-17 Instructional notes, video/DVD, and music CD for **Tanko Bushi** are included in *Multicultural Folk Dance Treasure Chest*, Volume 2. Instructional notes, video/DVD, and music CD for **Tokyo Dontaku**, are included in *Favorite Folk Dances of Kids and Teachers*, Volume 1 (see Note A-8 above).

A-18 Instructional notes, video/DVD, and music CD for **Virginia Reel** are found in *Favorite Folk Dances of Kids and Teachers,* Volume 5 (see Note A-8 above). Additionally any fiddler music recording will usually work for this dance.

A-19 Select several music selections (without lyrics) that illustrate variations in feelings. For example one piece should be festive and celebratory, another should be somber, another might be drumming or other percussive instrument sounds, while another might be environmental sounds. Play these different pieces as background while students prepare their dances. In this way they can pick one to accompany their dance if they choose to have accompaniment for it.

A-20 A drum or other rhythm instrument is extremely valuable during dance sessions to provide a rhythm and tempo for activities. Students also enjoy taking turns to play them and to accompany the class. A variety of striking and shaking rhythm instruments can usually be purchased at educational supply houses. These include drums, blocks, tambourines, triangles, bells, maracas, and hand cymbals or castanets. *Authentic Indian Dances and Folklore* (cited in A-16 above and available through Educational Record Center, 1-888-372-4543 or http://www.erckids.com) provides instructions for making rhythm instruments. It is important to use a variety of sounds to accompany dance activities. Sometimes students will have access to instruments from different cultures that can be introduced as well.

A-21 Dance sessions are good times to introduce poetry to students. Poetry suggests movement through its words and rhythm. Poets who have written for children and whose work can inspire creative movement responses include: Lewis Carroll, Bruce Lansky, Jack Prelutsky, Shel Silverstein, and Robert Louis Stevenson. Children also enjoy creating dances to poems written by other young people.

A-22 Dance sessions provide opportunities to not only connect with students' current reading across the curriculum, but also to introduce new reading sources. For example there are several books that could be incorporated with the map creating activity. For older students these might include Homer's *Odyssey* (retold by Robin Lister. 2004. Boston: Kingfisher Epics. Houghton Mifflin Co., Imprint) and *Robinson Crusoe* (Daniel Defoe. 2001. New York: Aladdin Paperbacks. Imprint of Simon and Schuster Children's Publishing Division). For younger students, *Grandfather's Journey* (Say, Allen. 1993. Boston and New York: Houghton Mifflin Company) recounts the trip a Japanese citizen made across America, and *The Little Prince* (De Saint-Exupéry, Antoine. English translation by Richard Howard. 2000. New York: Harcourt, Inc.) chronicles travels in space.

A-23 Using paintings as inspiration for creating dances, links dance with visual arts and artists. Art history books provide reproductions of contrasting (form, type, content) paintings from different time periods and a variety of geographical locations. For example from earlier times include replicas of cave drawings or Egyptian hieroglyphs. Select paintings throughout the ages that illustrate people or animals going about their daily lives. These are particularly useful if the paintings reflect an aesthetic or attitude of the time and place that can be illustrated in movement. In contrast also include examples of modern abstract painting. Jackson Pollock's work is particularly notable for students' movement creativity. Variety in visual art expressions provides opportunity for comparison and reflection on all art works as valid expressions of someone's feelings or ideas at some place at some time.

A-24 Dance activities should introduce students to music of all forms. Dance class may be the first and only time students hear instrumental music without lyrics. It may be the first and only time students hear music from other countries and cultures using different sounds and instruments. It may also be the only time students hear classical music. (Incidentally using music without lyrics or words helps students listen to the music as a form of expression rather than accepting meaning based on the spoken words.) Therefore variety in sound accompaniment should be an objective in dance lesson planning. There are both cultural and classical music collections designed for children available in educational music and book stores. For example *Boys Gotta Dance!* produced by Delos International, Inc. 2004, has classical music selections for children throughout. The Russian composer, Peter Ilyich Tchaikovsky, known as the composer of many ballets also composed several suites for children. Tchaikovsky's *Nutcracker Suite* and *Peter and the Wolf* by the Russian composer, Sergey Prokofiev, should both be part of the music experience of young people.

A-25 Sound effects can effectively accompany some dance activities. They can provide a background environment for a representative movement (such as a specific machine), they can provide a rhythm for movement, or can be used abstractly to create an unrelated movement. Students can create their own sound effects, record sound effects they hear everyday, or utilize commercially reproduced sound effects.

A-26 Preset marks in a circle on the floor are helpful for placing young children. "X" marks with masking tape will work, or anything that will not move so children will not slip or fall when standing or moving.

APPENDIX B

Additional Dance Lesson Plan Resources

Following are three types of resources: content and achievement standards to use as guidelines when planning lessons; sources of already prepared lessons for Pre-K/K, K–12, and differently-abled students; and sources of video and other materials to enhance lessons. Websites are included as applicable.

B-1 **Content and Achievement Standards to Use as Guidelines When Planning Lessons**

National Standards for Arts Education: Dance, Music, Theatre, and Visual Arts (1994). Reston, VA: Consortium of National Arts Education Associations. http://artsedge.kennedy-center.org/teach/standards.cfm. Also available for purchase through National Dance Education Organization: www.ndeo.org.

National Standards for Dance Education and Opportunity-to-Learn Standards in Dance Education. (1997). Reston, VA: National Dance Association. Available for purchase: www.aahperd.org/nda.

Standards for Dance in Early Childhood. (2002). Bethesda, MD: National Dance Education Organization. Available: www.ndeo.org.

Standards for Dance Learning and Teaching in the Arts: Ages 5-18. (2005). Bethesda, MD: National Dance Education Organization. Available: www.ndeo.org.

Moving into the Future: National Standards for Physical Education. (2004). Reston, VA: National Association for Sport and Physical Education. Available for purchase: www.naspeinfo.org.

B-2 **Sources of Already Prepared Dance Lessons**

John F. Kennedy Center for the Performing Arts Education Program dance lesson plans can be accessed based on grade level and curriculum focus (math, language arts, etc.) at http://artsedge.kennedy-center.org

All of the books and video listed below, containing already prepared lesson plans, can be purchased through the National Dance Association (www.aahperd.org/nda) or the National Dance Education Organization (www.nedo.org).

B-2-a Pre-K/K-6 Students

Cone, Theresa Purcell. (1994). *Teaching Children Dance: Becoming a Master Teacher.* Champaign, IL: Human Kinetics. Activities and lesson plans for Pre-K to grade 6.

Gilbert, Anne Green. (2002) *Teaching the Three R's Through Movement Experiences.* Bethesda, MD: NDEO. Movement activities aligned with K-6 academic curriculum.

Overby, Lynnette Young, Beth C. Post, and Diane Newman. (2005). *Interdisciplinary Learning through Dance: 101 MOVEntures.* Champaign, IL: Human Kinetics. Provides lesson plans for K-5 students.

Stinson, Susan. (1988). *Dance for Young Children: Finding the Magic in Movement.* Reston, VA: AAHPERD. Provides activities for ages 2 to 8.

B-2-b K-12 Students

Gilbert, Anne Green. (2003). *Brain Dance* (video). Reston, VA: AAHPERD. 85 minutes. Activities for all ages.

Gilbert, Anne Green. (1996). *Creative Dance for All Ages.* Reston, VA: AAHPERD. Lesson plans for all ages.

Lloyd, Marcia L. (1998) *Adventures in Creative Movement Activities: A Guide for Teaching.* (2nd Edition). Dubuque, IA: Eddie Bowers Publishing Co. Lessons for preschool through university.

McGreevy-Nichols, Susan, Helene Scheff, and Marty Sprague. (2001). *Building More Dances: Blueprints for Putting Movements Together.* Champaign, IL: Human Kinetics. Activities and lessons for K-12 students.

B-2-c Differently-abled Students

Dunkin, Anne. (1994). "Dancing with Dyslexic and Learning-Disabled Students." In *Dance Teacher Now.* 16, no. 4: pp. 54-58.

Dunphy, Kim and Jenny Scott. (2003). *Freedom to Move: Movement and Dances for People with Intellectual Disabilities.* Sydney, Australia: Maclennan and Petty, Limited.

Elin, Jane and Boni Boswell. (2004). *Re-envisioning Dance.* Reston, VA: AAHPERD.

McMahon, Patricia. (2000). *Dancing Wheels.* Boston, MA: Houghton Mifflin Co.

Two websites, www.axisdance.org and www.gggreg.com/dancingwheels.html, describe the work of two dance companies, Axis Dance in California and Dancing Wheels in Ohio, that include dancers with different abilities and disabilities in their dance performances and classes. Additionally the NDEO Research in Dance Education database cited in this text has reviews of research involving differently-abled populations in dance activity. Go to www.ndeo.org/research. Search "population served" category: differently-abled.

B-3 **Sources for Video and Other Materials to Enhance Lessons**

Princeton Book Company, 1-800-220-7149 or http://www.dancehorizons.com. stocks videos and other materials to enhance dance lessons, including the packages of instructional notes, videos/DVDs, and music CDs for the group dances described in this text: *Favorite Folk Dances of Kids and Teachers, Multicultural Folk Dance Treasure Chest; Dancetime II: 500 Years of Social Dance Volume II: 20th Century;* and *Hip Hop Kidz.*

Educational Record Center, 1-888-372-4543 or http://www.erckids.com stocks instructional packages with cassettes and guides for many dance activities for children, including *The Authentic Indian Dances and Folklore* cited in this text.

APPENDIX C

Dance Education Networking Resources

C-1 National and international organizations, listed below in alphabetical order, provide links to other arts organization.

Dance and the Child International (DaCi) www.daCiUsa.com

DaCi held its first conference in 1978 in Edmonton, Alberta and continues to sponsor a conference every four years at different locations around the world. Membership is open to all who are concerned with dance for children (to age eighteen). In 1997 DaCi USA members organized a national chapter, which plans programs, regional meetings, and publishes a newsletter for its members.

National Dance Association (NDA) www.aahperd.org/nda-about.html

NDA is one of several associations in the American Alliance for Health, Physical Education, Recreation, and Dance (AAHPERD). AAHPERD is the largest and oldest organization supporting those involved in physical education, leisure, fitness, dance, health promotion, and education. NDA, as an association in AAHPERD, has been in existence for almost eighty years. It sponsors an annual conference and regional meetings. Membership is open and members receive a journal, newsletters, and discounts on AAHPERD published documents. AAHPERD and NDA both have local organizations in many states.

National Dance Education Organization (NDEO) www.ndeo.org

Organized in 1998, NDEO works to promote dance education centered in the arts, to strengthen the national voice of dance education, and to assist states in their implementation of dance education. NDEO provides a link to more than 150 arts education related organizations and sponsors an annual conference and regional meetings. Membership, which is open, includes a quarterly journal, newsletters, discounts on dance education publications and access to the Research in Dance Education Database cited in this text. The database is also available through licensure to libraries, schools, and other research facilities. Additionally NDEO is involved in encouraging research projects in dance education.

C-2 The organization listed below is helpful in finding private dance studio recommendations.

National Registry of Dance Educators (NRDE) www.nrde.org

NRDE is a peer-evaluated membership organization organized in 1996. Formed with the intent of improving teaching standards in dance education, this organization of private dance studio dance educators hopes to educate the general public regarding excellence in dance education. This website can be used as a first step toward trying to locate dance studios in specific geographical locations.

C-3 State Organizations

Most states have dance alliances or associations, many of which are affiliated with one or more of the organizations listed above.

Additionally most states have an Alliance for Arts Education or similar organization. Such arts education organizations often work with a state's arts council. Arts education organizations keep members abreast of national and state legislation regarding arts education including dance.

About the Author

Anne Dunkin, M.A., University of Maryland, and PhD., University of California at Riverside, has been actively involved with children's dance education for many years. She cofounded the professional dance company Qwindo's Window which toured extensively for fourteen years, presenting dance programs to elementary school students. That experience involved working directly with arts organizations and state and local boards of education, Title I, and migrant worker education programs to develop performances and workshops for teachers and their students. She has taught dance at Landmark West School for dyslexic students in Encino, CA, at Gill St. Bernards School in Bernardsville, NJ, and dance for deaf students at Kendall Elementary School of Gallaudet College.

For ten years Dr. Dunkin was on the faculty of California State University at Fullerton, teaching "teaching dance" to preservice teachers, and has taught in studios in Washington, DC, New York and Los Angeles. Her articles on teaching dance have appeared in *Dance Teacher Now* and *Arts Education Policy Review*. She currently serves as Coordinator for the Research in Dance Education database at the National Dance Education Organization.